THE BRAZEN SERPENT

CHAOS AND ORDER

M. R. Osborne

Foreword by Alistair Lees

Rose Circle Books

Third Edition

Rose Circle Publications, 2025

A catalogue for this book is available from the British Library

Copyright © M. R. Osborne 2021, 2022, 2025

All rights reserved. No part of this book may be reproduced, distributed, stored in a retrieval system, or transmitted in any form or by any means, including photocopying, recording, or other electronic or mechanical methods, without the prior written permission of the publisher, except in the case of brief quotations embodied in critical reviews and certain other non-commercial uses permitted by copyright law.

For permission requests, write to the publisher at the address below.

Paperback ISBN: 978-1-0684008-2-7

Rose Circle Publications
P.O. Box 854
Bayonne, NJ 07002, U.S.A.
www.rosecirclebooks.com

Contents

Foreword	1
Introduction	5
1. Number and the Brazen Serpent	21
2. Nehushtan	81
3. Dunamis	111
4. The Tree of Life	139
5. The Omega Point	181
Selected Bibliography	197
Index	201

Foreword to the First Edition

This is the third published work of M. R. Osborne's innermost thoughts, and another good example of his enquiring mind. He previously brought us Pasqually's esoteric teachings in the first English translation of the *Lessons of Lyon* and the incredible images, and the new insight found in his second book *The Most Holy Trinosophia: A Book of the Dead*. I have known the author for only four years and yet he has made quite an impression in such a short space of time. I pride myself in being actively involved with encouraging him to write and deliver his Metropolitan College S.R.I.A. study group paper on Martinez de Pasqually in December 2017, which led to him acquiring the Companion of Christian Rosenkreutz Award.

This was while he was finishing the translations of his epic book, the first published English translation of the *Lessons of Lyon* on the esoteric teachings of Martinez de Pasqually, written for his two famous students in 1774-76. His translation also includes some of Pasqually's letters and is the first to use illustrations from that period for some of these lessons. Both Pasqually and Saint-Martin's thoughts are interwoven into the narrative of this book and specifically Pasqually's opinions on the *Prima materia*. M. R. Osborne's Martinist pedigree shines through his thoughts and new ideas and I was very pleased to be asked to write the foreword.

His latest work begins by lifting the lid on some of his innermost thoughts on the divine code found in nature, and the numbers that he sees in his everyday life. He compares these correspondences with other authors and links these significantly with the divine code found behind the Brazen Serpent or Nehushtan, which first comes to light when Moses raises a wooden cross with a brazen serpent and it successfully stave off a plague of serpents, that is mentioned in the Bible during the Children of Light's sojourn in the desert before arriving in the promised land.

The explanation of the significance of looking upon this first healing cross is nicely broken down into very interesting, illustrated sections explaining the act of raising a wooden cross by Moses, which he expands in later chapters on the Christian parallels with the crucifixion. The unexpected significance of the brazen serpent on its own, which was a very invocative ancient symbol in many old religions, alludes to wisdom and eternity of the Soul, in living creatures, because of the shedding of its skin. Followed by the importance of the combination of the cross and the serpent, linked with the healing power gratis of the cross a fundamental Rosicrucian aspiration, are all explained further in detail. The subject of the Nehushtan was new to me, in fact, I was glad to find that I was not alone in not really appreciating what the Nehushtan was or what it meant. I must admit that I do not consciously remember ever hearing its name mentioned at all, even though I am actively involved in parallel research of my own on the Brazen Serpent and Moses, now helped considerably by this book.

Some of the specific Christian beliefs expressed here are a little lost on me as a perennial philosopher, believing in the parallel merits of all religions, but they are appreciated by me and no doubt by his audience on their own merits. I was also not expecting the Christian aspects of this wooden cross in the desert, more than a thousand years before the association with the crucifixion but can now see how both can be linked to a form of the Burning Bush and God's presence therein as an aspect of the Tree of life and why it was not consumed by fire. The significance of the Serpent in the Garden of Eden and the fall, combined with the ancient symbol of the *Serpent* and the *Wooden Cross* as the healing Nehu-shtan, a precursor of the *Crucifixion*, where Christ is ultimately raised on a similarly shaped cross to heal all mankind and as he will become, born again for those who follow, and he explains why.

Not only does M. R. Osborne use numerology and alchemy to illustrate other examples of these Rosicrucian-like correspondences, but he also uses the words of many more modern philosophers in the narrative. He cites sacred geometry and other meaningful images that are used by others to explain these Divine lessons. Like most people, I am enthralled by Egyptian thoughts and ideas that are expressed by the author, who explains many of the Egyptian symbols behind the Nehushtan in this book. Some of this research no doubt coming from his second book *The Most Holy Trinosophia : A Book of the Dead*, which is a brand-new insight into Alessandro di Cagliostro's work, a French esoteric book sometimes erroneously credited to the Comte de Saint-Germain, and like this, a brave new approach to old ways of thinking. I cannot praise enough an author who is prepared to give a little of themselves and offer new insights and thoughts on old subjects, especially if they can break new ground and open up the audience's mind to these new ideas, in my opinion.

Alistair McGawn Lees
Author of *The English Illuminati*
Librarian General of the S.R.I.A.
November, 2021

Introduction

> *There is no magic curse against Jacob and no divination against Israel. It will now be said about Jacob and Israel what great things God has done.*
> Numbers 23:23

The theme of this work is simple: an exploration of the myth of the Brazen Serpent as a cipher for the "Divine Code" concealed within everything about us. This short book is therefore an odyssey, an eventful journey through the hidden paths of numerology, geometry, and allegory, amongst other things. It is not lengthy, despite that journey being the oldest and longest. Indeed, it is as much about what is omitted as what is included in these pages since it is your task to find meaning and truth in the world about you. That is the lonely path of the self-initiate, but one we must all travel eventually.

Setting the Scene

The events of the Old Testament are allegories (stories, poems, and images) which reveal hidden moral or spiritual meanings to adepts of any faith or none. Likewise, behind the mystery and symbolism of the occult lies the phenomenological Divine Code embedded in the fabric of time and space. Thus, the history of the Jewish people from the Exodus to the advent of Christ is but a chapter in the alchemical Book of Man.

Our journey begins with exploring the power and characteristics of numbers, which is key to understanding the Divine Code and the sacred geometry it forms. Without this understanding, the mystery and concealed truth of the Nehushtan cannot be fully understood. The esotericist Louis-Claude de Saint-Martin summarised it thus:

> "Now, we have the prerogative of forming, after the similitude of the All-Wise, an indissoluble, eternal alliance between our minds and our sacred hearts, by uniting them in the principle which formed them; and it is only on this indispensable condition that we can hope to become again the images of God; and in striving for this, our conviction is confirmed, as to the painful fact of our degradation, and, at the same time, of our superiority over the external order."[1]

The name "Nehushtan" for the Brazen Serpent occurs only once in the Bible, at the time of Hezekiah's religious reforms in the sixth century BC. The root meaning in Hebrew is *nahash* ("to raise up"), which can also mean intuitive knowledge and/or natural ability. The Hebrew phrase *nahash nehoshet* means a "bronze [or brazen] serpent". Since *nahash* relates to the Biblical word for snake, the name Nehushtan in 2 Kings should be interpreted as "the Raised Brazen Serpent".

---

[1] Saint-Martin, L-C. de, *Man: His True Nature & Ministry* (Trans. Edward Burton Penny, London, 1864) p.24.

Israel's chapter in the Book of Man is critical since the Brazen Serpent in the Biblical book of Numbers is a Messianic prototype, a foreshadowing of Christ's coming, and the harmonisation of the opposite forms of nature and spirit.

The setting for exploring this Divine Code begins along the winding, serpentine path taken by the Hebrews during their long years in the wilderness of the Sinai, sometime during the fourteenth century BC. It was at Qadesh ("the Fountain of Judgement") near modern day Ain el-Qudeirat in the Sinai, that the most severe judgement on the unfaithful Israelites took place:

> "I have forgiven them, as you asked. Nevertheless, as surely as I live and as surely as the glory of the Lord fills the whole earth, not one of those who saw my glory and the signs I performed in Egypt and in the wilderness but who disobeyed me and tested me ten times— not one of them will ever see the land I promised on oath to their ancestors. No one who has treated me with contempt will ever see it." Numbers 14:20-23

This brutal judgement prefigures the curious story of the Brazen Serpent, appearing as it does amid other strange events recorded in the Book of Numbers:

- Moses' sister, the prophet Miriam, dies (Numbers 20:1);
- the Israelites argue with Moses about the lack of water. The "Waters of Strife" incident then takes place at Meribah, when Moses miraculously strikes

a rock for water but fails to acknowledge God (Exodus 17:1-7);
- the Hebrews are refused passage through Edom, an ancient kingdom located in the barren Negev Desert (Numbers 20:14-21);
- Moses' brother, the High Priest Aaron, ascends Mount Hor in the area south of the Dead Sea to ordain his son, and dies at the age of 123 on the summit (Numbers 20:22-29); and
- departing, the people are forced to detour around Edom, and in anger plot a return to Egypt.

Moses receives regulations for the consecration, Hans Holbein the Younger, 1538

"And the people spake against God, and against Moses, wherefore have ye brought us up out of Egypt to die in the wilderness? for there is no bread, neither is there any water; and our soul loatheth this light bread." Numbers 21:5

In response to this continuous infidelity, God is said to have sent a plague of "fiery serpents" to punish the people, whose venomous bites kill many of them:

> "And the Lord sent fiery serpents among the people, and they bit the people; and many people of Israel died." Numbers 21:6

In an act of repentance, the Hebrews approach Moses to intercede on their behalf. God then commands Moses:

> "Make thee a brazen serpent and set it upon a pole; and it shall come to pass, that every one that is bitten, when he seeth it, shall live."

Numbers 21:4-9 There is no physical description of the Brazen Serpent in the Bible. The reappearance of the icon in 2 Kings 18:4 (referred to in a possibly disparaging way as "the Nehushtan"[2]) states that, several hundred years after the events described at Edom, King Hezekiah of Judah removed it from the Temple courtyard and broke it up:

> "He removed the high places, and break the images, and cut down the groves, and brake in pieces the brazen serpent that Moses had made: for unto those days the children of Israel did burn incense to it: and he called it Nehushtan." 2 Kings 18:4

---

[2] Lit. "Raised Brazen Serpent."

Moses at the Burning Bush by Hans Holbein the Younger

There is similarly no description of the Brazen Serpent in the Gospel of John, despite Christ being identified with it:

> "And as Moses lifted up the serpent in the wilderness, even so must the son of man be lifted up: that whosoever believeth in him should not perish but have eternal life." John 3:14-15

So, it cannot be said with any certainty that the staff comprised the form of the Hebrew letter tau (a cross shape in ancient times), as is often depicted in sacred art. An example of this impression of the Nehushtan appears in the sculpture erected by the Franciscans at Mount Nebo, near Eilat in the Negev, on the northern tip of the Red Sea.

The Tau

The tau is the final and twenty-second letter of the Hebrew alphabet. Derived from the Phoenicians, it was originally a pictograph of two crossed sticks. The Zohar applies "the four sparks of godliness" to the tau, an allusion perhaps to the classical elements of fire, wind, earth and water, believed to be the signature of God embedded in the universe. In Jewish tradition the letter represents the word *emes* ("truth").

The Hebrews regarded the tau as a sign of the covenant and, thus, became a token or sigil of God's power over life and death. The following passage from the book of Ezekiel is interesting since it describes the prophet's vision of the destruction of Jerusalem by the "heavenly executioners", who were only to spare those who wore the mark of the tau:

"'Go all through Jerusalem and mark a "tau" on the foreheads of all who deplore and disapprove of all the evil practices in the city.'

The memorial plaque at the foot of the Eilat Nehushtan reads: "The Law was given through Moses; grace and truth came through Jesus Christ." John 1:17

I heard him say to the others, 'Follow him through the city and strike. Show neither pity nor mercy, kill and exterminate them all. But do not touch anyone with the sign of the tau.'" Ezekiel 9:4

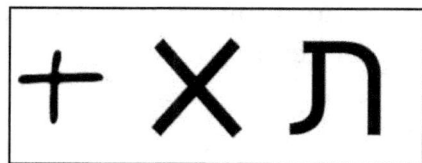

The evolution of the letter tau *from the Phoenician to the modern Hebrew alphabet*

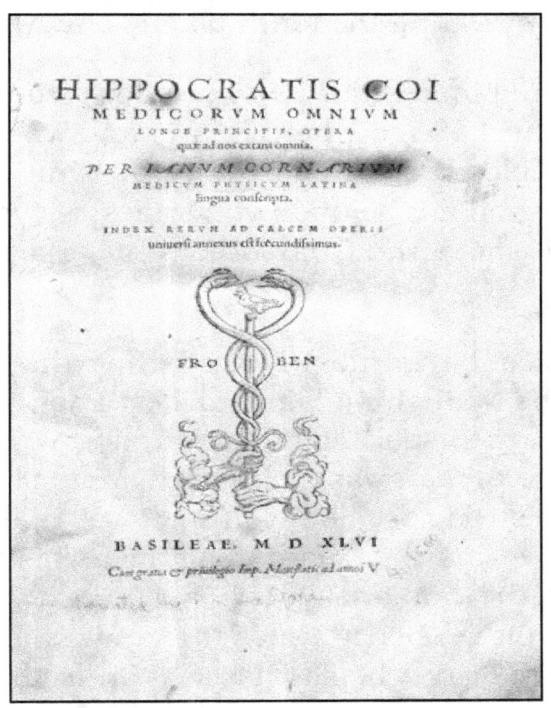

The Crusaders considered the tau a symbol of healing because they believed the Brazen Serpent had been affixed to a staff in the shape of a cross. The idea that the symbol prefigures Christ was not new, as we shall discover, and plays a large part in the Messianic symbolism contained in the Brazen Serpent myth. This also helps explain the form of the Nehushtan as depicted in specific high-grade masonic orders today, which owes its origins to the initiatory rites and symbolism of the medieval craft guilds infiltrated by Crusader artisans.

Yet, as tantalising and evocative as this image appears, there is nothing in the Biblical narrative to support its having been used to suspend the Serpent, although it is suggestive of the blood-mark in the account of the Angel of Death during the tenth plague of Egypt:

> "And the blood shall be to you for a token upon the houses where ye are: and when I see the blood, I will pass over you, and the plague shall not be upon you to destroy you, when I smite the land of Egypt." Exodus 12:13

It should also be borne in mind that the Biblical account of the Nehushtan is the earliest known *written* record of a serpent-pole combination, and while there is no evidence the tau was incorporated into it, I would regard it as a strong possibility. If so, it was understood as a collective mark of pardon or mercy, and as a reminder of the immanence of God in nature. It is interesting that in ancient times the tau was used as a symbol for life or death. The association of the raised serpent on a cross has long been established with the medical profession. Here it appears on the cover of one of the first books of medicine, printed in 1546, the *Hippocratis Coi Medicorum Omnium.*

The tau cross also appears in the Tarot. Whilst Tarot cards are still commonly used for conventional card games, in the English-speaking world they are reserved almost exclusively for occult use and divination. The Hanged Man is the twelfth card in the Major Arcana of the Tarot deck, and depicts an image of a man being hanged upside-down from his left foot.

The tree from which he hangs is in the shape of a tau. A,E. Waite suggested that the image represents "life in suspension."

> "I will say very simply on my own part that it expresses the relation, in one of its aspects, between the Divine and the Universe. He who can understand that the story of his higher nature is imbedded in this symbolism will receive intimations concerning a great awakening that is possible and will know

that after the sacred Mystery of Death there is a glorious Mystery of Resurrection."[3]

These are significant claims but suggestive of God's Real Presence in nature. Although the suspended man is in a position where he is unable to control his situation, at the same time he is conscious of it. Indeed, the hanged man purposefully crosses his right leg, to form either a fylfot cross or the Hebrew letter lamed (ל). The significance of the heraldic fylfot is geometric since it is a cross with four perpendicular extensions at 90° angles. The lamed is the twelfth letter in the Hebrew alphabet, and its appearance in the twelfth Major Arcana in the Tarot cannot be coincidental. It must indeed reflect the Biblical use of the tau as a token to distinguish the repentant from the unrepentant.

However. The tau as a mark was also used to protect the reprobate Cain:

> "And the Lord said unto him: 'Therefore whosoever slayeth Cain, vengeance shall be taken on him sevenfold.' And the Lord set a mark upon Cain, lest any finding him should kill him. And the Lord said unto him, 'Therefore whosoever slayeth Cain, vengeance shall be taken on him sevenfold.'"
> Genesis 4:15

---

[3] A.E. Waite, *The Pictorial Key to the Tarot* (London 1910).

In the book of Revelation, the tau again features as a seal or mark, this time to be placed on those who are to be spared the suffering of the Armageddon:

> "And I saw another angel ascending from the east, having the seal of the living God: and he cried with a loud voice to the four angels, to whom it was given to hurt the earth and the sea, saying, 'Hurt not the earth, neither the sea, nor the trees, till we have sealed the servants.'" Revelation 7:2-3

More curious still, is the account in *The Trial of the Vowels* by the ancient Greek satirist Lucian of Samosata (AD 125 – 180), who composed a comedic "trial" of the vowel letters by the consonants. In the trial, the Greek letter Sigma accuses the Hebrew tau of inventing the model for crucifixion, i.e. suffering, and demands it be executed in its own shape:

> "Men weep, and bewail their lot, and curse Cadmus with many curses for introducing Tau into the family of letters; they say it was his body that tyrants took for a model, his shape that they imitated, when they set up the erections on which men are crucified."[4]

The Fiery Ones

The account in Numbers 21:6-9 uses the Hebrew word *seraph* to describe Moses' Raised Serpent. The attacking snakes are also described as *seraphim*, meaning "fiery serpents". The seraphim also feature in

---

[4] *The Works of Lucian of Samosata*, Fowler H.W. & Fowler F.G. (Tr.) Oxford, 1905. Vol. 1, p.30.

the Bible as winged angelic beings. The supernatural seraphim of the Old Testament are the spiritual entities of the first emanation of God, many of whom rebelled against the Creator and, in turn, became demons. Their role in the narrative was the persecution of the unruly Hebrews, which is why Moses' Raised Serpent only provided relief and did not banish or destroy these demonic forces.

It is therefore possible that the Nehushtan may have been portrayed as a winged, angelic seraph. In any event, the seraphim attacking the people in the desert may well have flown:

> "Rejoice not thou, whole Palestina, because the rod of him that smote thee is broken: for out of the serpent's root shall come forth a cockatrice, and his fruit shall be a fiery flying serpent." Isaiah 14:29

> "The burden of the beasts of the south: into the land of trouble and anguish, from whence come the young and old lion, the viper and fiery flying serpent, they will carry their riches upon the shoulders of young asses, and their treasures upon the bunches of camels, to a people that shall not profit them." Isaiah 30:6

There is, however, no description of the Raised Serpent in scripture. It is pure conjecture to imagine its likely appearance as a winged seraph. Hidden within the myth of the Brazen Serpent, however, is the meaning of the numbers, codes and geometric patterns through which God conceals himself in nature.

The Raised Serpent of Moses was a visual cipher of spirit locked in physical matter. In short, the Divine Code is there to be discovered.

M. R. Osborne, M.A.
Northampton, November 2021

1 | Number and the Brazen Serpent

"The path to paradise begins in hell"
Dante Alighieri

Exodus

Written sometime around the fifth century BC, the Biblical book of Exodus describes the deliverance myth of the Hebrews. The disgraced Moses, forced to depart Egypt on a charge of murder, experiences an epiphany of God and is commanded to liberate the enslaved people "chosen" to be covenanted with God. If he existed at all, and is not an entirely mythological character, the Biblical narrative tells us that Moses was born to Levite parents.[5] During the Egyptian bondage, the Levites were exempted from labour and devoted themselves to spiritual pursuits on the premise of their descent from Jacob's third son, Levi, of whom it was written of their zealous religious temperament:

> "Cursed be their anger, for it was fierce; and their wrath, for it was cruel: I will divide them in Jacob and scatter them in Israel." Genesis 49:6-7

---

[5] "And there went a man of the house of Levi and took to wife a daughter of Levi." Exodus 2:1.

The name Levi is derived from the Hebrew "he shall accompany". The name Moses however is from the Egyptian given name Mesu, meaning "son". Mesu is often used with lofty titles bearing the name of a god, such as Rameses (Ra-Moses, son of Ra) or Thutmose (Tut-Moses, son of Thoth).

The story of Moses follows a familiar motif found in other near eastern accounts of a leader abandoned at birth and rising from water. For example, the first ruler of the Akkadian Empire in the 23rd century BC, Sargon the Great's origins were detailed as follows:

> "My mother, the high priestess, conceived; in secret she bore me She set me in a basket of rushes, with bitumen she sealed my lid She cast me into the river which rose over me."[6]
> Sargon the Great

In exile and while summiting Mount Horeb as a shepherd, Moses is stunned to see "the angel of the Lord appearing in a flame of fire, out of the midst of a bush that did not burn" (Exodus 3:2). The voice of God speaks through the angel (seraph) within the burning bush commanding Moses to return to Egypt to set his people free. Moses is reluctant to return, and asks God for power, so that the people will believe and follow his leadership. In a sense Moses fails a test of faith. God's response both terrifies and emboldens him. In the form of a seemingly innocuous question God asks: "What is that in thine hand?" (Exodus 4:2). Moses, who holds a shepherd's staff, simply replies "a wooden rod" (and

---

[6] M. Siebeck, *Forschungen zum Alten Testament* (Trans. T. D. Finlay, London 2005). p. 236.

may as well have caustically quipped, "Why, what do you think it looks like?"). God then tells him to cast the staff on the ground and it then transmutes into a living, terrifying serpent. This magical operation is reversed by Moses, when he is commanded by God to pick it up:

> "Moses, put forth thine hand and take it by the tail. And he put forth his hand and caught it, and it became a rod in his hand."
> Exodus 4:4

What Moses picks up is no longer a simple shepherd's crook, but a magi's wand. He overcomes his instinctive fear in his desire to obey God, for the "serpent" must have been venomous. We can see how the wooden staff and the living serpent merge, the latter being immanent within the wand. The serpent-wand is now a living form of God's power; since what was once made of dead wood is now imbued with the living *prima materia* or fifth element of spirit within. It will be recalled that the incident occurs on a raised mountainous location, and so we have a prototype of the Nehushtan already, in the form of the staff.

It is worth recalling that the Egyptian kings carried croziers and wore uraei snakes as headdress decorations. In the Americas, the diadem of the kings represented the tail of the *Xiuhcoatl*, the fire serpent deity of the Aztecs. The *Xiuhcoatli* were regarded as protective deities and portrayed as weapons. Serpent worship also formed a large element of ancient Canaanite religion in the Bronze Age (approximately 3300 BC to 1200 BC). Snake cult objects have been discovered at several settlements, most notably two bronze serpent statues at the site of the Canaanite temple at Megiddo.[7] The Minoans, Hittites, Babylonians and Assyrians were all believed to have venerated bronze statues of gods holding a serpent and a staff.

The Brazen Serpent by Benjamin West (1738-1820)

---

[7] M. Münnich, *The Cult of Bronze Serpents in Ancient Canaan and Israel*, World Union of Jewish Studies, 2005, pp. 39-56.

British Museum (author's photograph)

Serpent worship was also widespread in Egypt, and the goddess Wadjet was depicted as a cobra or uraei. The pharaohs also created mountains of stone and pyramids upon which they could be raised. These were separate forms, of course, whereas Moses' wand combined all these qualities within itself, albeit that it appeared as a shepherd's rod. His wand represented the harmonised aspects of the forces it represented:

> "And thou shalt take this rod in thine hand, wherewith thou shalt do signs." Exodus 4:17

These forces corresponded with God's glory and the Hebrews' spiritual happiness, which were so closely connected that one necessarily needed the other. Despite the iniquitous attempts of the Egyptian Government to make the people suffer, they could now draw nearer to the source of God's felicity immanent within the staff Moses brought down from Mount Horeb, and which was essentially the burning bush itself, wherein the Divine communicated his thought, will and action on the elemental plane:

> "God said to Moses, 'I AM who I AM.' And he said, 'Say this to the people of Israel, I AM has sent me to you.'" Exodus 3:14

The burning bush was symbolic of the foundry ovens or fires by which the alchemists of ancient Egypt strove to perfect the elemental world through the smelting of bronze and the assaying of gold. The word alchemy, Kimiya, is thought to be derived from the Egyptian name for the country's fertile black soil.

Metallurgy was an attempt to discover the life force in the *prima materia* of nature, and therefore fire symbolised the Living Substance in material matter. It follows that the tree was not destroyed in the burning bush because this was no ordinary, physical fire. The fire was the very Substance of God himself, the *prima materia* from which everything in creation had been made. We will recall that the Hebrew word for angel is seraph, which derives from the plural seraphim, or "fiery ones". Seraph is also synonymous with the Hebrew word for fiery snake or fiery serpent.

So, it carries a dual meaning for both natural and supernatural beings, which begs the question whether the angelic forms may resemble fiery serpents, or perhaps flashes of lightening? An interesting thought if we consider the description of the Tempter as a serpent in the Garden of Eden.

Moses Receives the Tablets of the Law, Hans Holbein the Elder

In Hebrew, letters are also used as numbers, which is known as Gematria. Gematria is a form of numerology, where the first ten letters are given values that increase consecutively from one to ten. The next eight letters are given number values that increase by a factor of ten from twenty to ninety, and the final four letters are given number values that increase by a factor of one hundred to four hundred. So, for example, the Hebrew letter aleph is one, bet is two, and the letter gimel equates to the three, which means to be raised up, or pride. The tau corresponds to four hundred. Gematria is also essential to Hebrew Kaballah, which adheres to a cosmological system based on the creation of the universe by God, through the acoustic sound of certain Hebrew letters and their numerical values. The seraphim and the Nehushtan alike therefore both have numerological values in Hebraic Kaballah.

When Moses and Aaron encounter Pharaoh to demand the release of the Hebrews, the initial response is a request for a supernatural sign, i.e., prove your authority! This was not an unreasonable request and is analogous to Moses asking God for magical powers before the burning bush. This, as we know, resulted in the transformation of the shepherd's crook into a magi's wand.

> "And the Lord spake unto Moses and unto Aaron, saying, When Pharaoh shall speak unto you, saying, 'Show a miracle' to you: then thou shalt say unto Aaron, 'Take thy rod, and cast it before Pharaoh, and it shall become a serpent.' And Moses and Aaron went in unto Pharaoh, and they did so as the Lord had commanded: and Aaron cast down his rod before Pharaoh, and before his servants, and it became a serpent. Then Pharaoh also called the wise men and the sorcerers: now the magicians of Egypt, they also did in like manner with their enchantments. For they cast down every man his rod, and they became serpents: but

Aaron's rod swallowed up their rods."
Exodus 7:8-13

Moses and Aaron before Pharoah

In this passage, another serpent emerges, this time from Aaron's staff. The serpent-staves of Moses and Aaron symbolise the branches of the Tree of Life in its axis with heaven and earth. In Egypt, the staff or crozier of Pharaoh was a metaphor for the king, who derived his authority from a divine source. Consequently, this encounter would have deeply troubled the Egyptians. That said, they will have identified Moses' and Aaron's serpent-staves with their deities and, being leery of a known murderer making demands damaging to their slave-based economy, refused them. Equally, they may have identified the staves with Apep, the serpentine-like deity of evil. The consequence of this decision led to discord, suffering and death within Egypt, in the form of the ten plagues. At the tenth and most dreadful plague, the book of Exodus recounts how the Hebrews survived by the use of operative magic to protect themselves from the most feared seraph of them all – the Angel of Death:

> "Speak ye unto all the congregation of Israel, saying, In the tenth day of this month they shall take to them every man a lamb, according to the house of their fathers, a lamb for an house ... And ye shall keep it up until the fourteenth day of the same month: and the whole assembly of the congregation of Israel shall kill it in the evening .... And they shall take of the blood and strike it on the two side posts and on the upper door post of the houses, wherein they shall eat it.... And ye shall let nothing of it remain until the morning; and that which remaineth of it until the morning ye shall burn with fire .... For I will pass through the land of Egypt this night and will smite all the firstborn in the land of Egypt, both man and beast; and against all the gods of Egypt I will execute judgement: I am the Lord ... And the blood shall be to you for a token upon the houses where ye are: and when I see the blood, I will pass over you, and the plague shall not be upon you to destroy you, when I smite the land of Egypt." Exodus 12:1-28

The first nine plagues are formed into three distinct groups. In the first, the Egyptians experience the power of God; in the second, God is directing events; and in the third, his superiority is displayed. The tenth is not in sequence because it is the plague of death. Interestingly, the length of time from the first to the last plague is twenty-three days, culminating with the death of the firstborn of Egypt on the twenty-third day. On the fourteenth day, the Israelites are told to prepare for the plague of the death. As we have seen, the number fourteen equates with the number five, which has a dual meaning, and in this context equates with suffering and death for the Egyptians and a corresponding freedom of the Hebrews.

Aaron and Hur holding up Moses' hands

Upon departing, these dual themes continue when the people are led by "the Angel of the Lord" in the form of a pillar of cloud by day, and a pillar of fire at night. Moses uses his serpent-wand to part the Red Sea to open a middle passage between the waters, thereby manipulating physical nature and in the process destroying the scourge of would-be killers in pursuit.

The Brazen Serpent

The fixing of a bronze or copper serpent to a pole is therefore symbolic of the Presence of the Living God. There is an interesting parallel with the Ark of the Covenant as well, which was partly made of natural wood and partly of metal. It is said that the Skekinah or Spirit of God dwelt within the Ark. The Ark was created by the craftsman Bezalel on the instruction of Moses, following God's command for there to be a place for Divine habitation on earth:

> "Have them make an Ark of acacia wood—two and a half cubits long, a cubit and a half wide, and a cubit and a half high! Overlay it with pure gold, both inside and out, and make a gold moulding around it. Cast four gold rings for it and fasten them to its four feet, with two rings on one side and two rings on the other. Then make poles of acacia wood and overlay them with gold. Insert the poles into the rings on the sides of the ark to carry it. The poles are to remain in the rings of this ark; they are not to be removed. Then put in the ark the tablets of the covenant law, which I will give you. Make an atonement cover of pure gold—two and a half cubits long and a cubit and a half wide. And make two cherubim out of hammered gold at the ends of the cover. Make one cherub on

one end and the second cherub on the other; make the cherubim of one piece with the cover, at the two ends. The cherubim are to have their wings spread upward, overshadowing the cover with them. The cherubim are to face each other, looking toward the cover. Place the cover on top of the ark and put in the ark the tablets of the covenant law that I will give you. There, above the cover between the two cherubim that are over the ark of the covenant law, I will meet with you and give you all my commands for the Israelites." Exodus 25:10-22

The Parting of the Red Sea, Sherry Adkins, wood burning and pencil

The Ark was a chest of acacia wood, which was gold-plated and lined. Acacia is a high-density wood of a reddish-brown colour, often described as the hardest wood used in carpentry. The fibres in the wood point in towards each other and are resistant to friction. Four gold rings were attached to the bottom of the chest, through which two staves were passed. These were also made of acacia and coated in gold. Two winged seraphim made of gold were placed on top, facing one another. There is therefore a curious symmetry with the Brazen Serpent and this description of the Ark, which, when combined with the immanent Presence of God within, adds a particular nuance to the meaning attributed to it. First, these are both objects combining wood and forged metal. Second, they share the imagery of the sacred staff; third, both contain seraph icons. Fourth, as we have seen, they both contain the hidden Presence of God within (since both may be said to be representations of the burning bush). When God communicated with Moses in the presence of the Ark, he did so from between the two seraphim (known as "the Mercy Seat"):

> "And when Moses was gone into the tabernacle of the congregation to speak with him, then he heard the voice of one speaking unto him from off the Mercy Seat that was upon the ark of testimony, from between the two cherubim: and he spake unto him."
> Numbers 7:89

God's command in respect of the raising of the Nehushtan also echoes that of the Ark:

> "And the Lord said unto Moses, make thee a fiery serpent, and set it upon a pole; and it shall come to pass, that every one that is bitten, when he looketh upon it, shall live." Numbers 21:8

It will be recalled that the plague of seraphim or snakes was a sign of God's displeasure with the unfaithful people, since his protection had been withdrawn as a punishment:

> "And the Lord sent fiery serpents among the people, and they bit the people; and much people of Israel died. Therefore the people came to Moses, and said, we have sinned, for we have spoken against the Lord, and against thee; pray unto the Lord, that he take away the serpents from us." (Numbers 21:6-7)

The corresponding sign of the return of God's dispensation to the people occurs with the advent of the Raised Serpent. God reassured Moses that anyone bitten by the fiery serpents would be saved upon looking at the brazen serpent on the pole. One cannot help but conclude that this equates with the Mercy Seat on the Ark of the Covenant, where the two serpents or winged angelic seraphim face one another, and from which God communicates his will to Moses.

> "And Moses made a serpent of brass, and set it upon a pole, and it came to pass, that if a serpent had bitten any man when he beheld the serpent of brass, he lived." Numbers 21:9

The raised pole is interesting, as we find a parallel passage in Exodus 17:8-12, where a hostile army of Amalekites confronts the Hebrews. Moses ascends a mountain to observe the fighting, and when he raises his staff the Israelites prevail, but whenever he lowers it, the Amalekites gain the upper hand. This is, again, another connection with the forces concealed within the Nehushtan. The Mishnah *Rosh HaShanah* also links the narrative of the Amalekite fighting with the Nehushtan:[8]

> "It may be asked: did the hands of Moses make war when he raised them or break war when he lowered them? Rather, the verse comes to tell you that as long as the Jewish people turned their eyes upward and subjected their hearts to their Father in Heaven, they prevailed, but if not, they fell. Similarly, you can say: The verse states: 'Make for yourself a fiery serpent, and set it upon a pole; and it shall come to pass, that everyone that is bitten, when he sees it, he shall live' (Numbers 21:8). Once again it may be asked: Did the serpent kill, or did the serpent preserve life? Rather, when the Jewish people turned their eyes upward and subjected their hearts to their Father in Heaven, they were healed, but if not, they rotted from their snakebites."[9]

---

[8] Mishnah Rosh HaShanah (3:8).
[9] Commentary on Mishnah Rosh HaShanah 1:1 (from sefaria.org).

Moses showing the Brazen Serpent, 30 August 1793, after Benjamin West

In light of the above, a few points are worth emphasising at this point. Firstly, Moses's serpent-wand, the Ark of the Covenant, and the Brazen Serpent are each comprised of dead/natural and living / supernatural forms. In Egyptian alchemy, the fifth element was the quintessence, the pure and essential essence created from chaos (Nun). It was regarded as a vital life force or ether, that could be manipulated through magic and the assaying of metals and other elemental forms. The four primary elements in nature and the fifth element of the *prima materia* are combined in the staff of Moses. Wood, in and of itself, grows in the earth, is nurtured by the fire / light of the sun, is fed by water and grows in the air. These elements recombine into the *tria prima,* or primal trinity of fire and air, air and water, and earth and water.

This is representative of the soul or igniting force, the spirit or mediating force that carries the soul into the body, and the body or integrating force combining soul and spirit into form. We might think of this along the lines of a serpentine-like lightning bolt. On a quantum level, it is through these forces and essentials that all matter and forms are generated. The significance of the dead wood in the staff, Ark and Nehushtan tells us that death is a process of the change of form, from one stage of alchemical transformation to another.

Secondly, the serpent-wand of Moses and the Ark undoubtedly symbolise the burning bush – the presence of God amongst the people. Thirdly, the pole used to raise the Brazen Serpent may symbolise both Moses' staff, which are later replicated in the two staves of the Ark, symbolising the power of God over life and death. The Brazen Serpent affixed to it projects supernatural and elemental power combined. In much the same way as the people can be cured by looking up to the Brazen Serpent, so they can be killed by touching the Ark:

> "And when they came unto the threshing floor of Chidon, Uzza put forth his hand to hold the ark; for the oxen stumbled. And the anger of the Lord was kindled against Uzza, and he smote him, because he put his hand

to the ark: and there he died before God."
(1 Chronicles 13:9-10)

Fourthly, God commands that the serpent and pole are to be raised, which mirrors both the Tree of Life and the Tree of Knowledge of Good and Evil in Genesis. The triune powers of Moses' staff that the pole symbolises remind us of the three branches of the Kabbalistic Tree of Life – namely the Pillars of Judgement, Mercy and Balance.

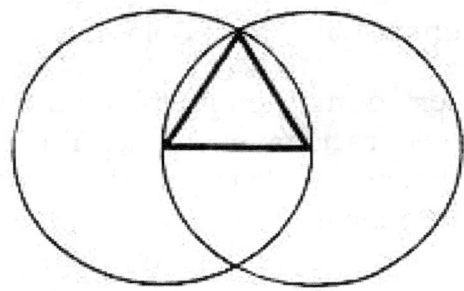

In geometrical terms, the vesica piscis (formed by two) intersected by the triangle (or three, formed by two) represents the perfect balance of two opposite forms with a third mediating form, for example, a trinity of man's mind, body and spirit. The opposing two and three is the numerological number five in all its aspects, as allegorised by the serpent-staff bringing plague to Egypt, the Ark striking dead the profane, and the plague of fiery serpents. The conjecture is that the Nehushtan is a disguised form of the vesica piscis converging with the geometric triangle, representing the fifth element trapped in elemental nature. The Nehushtan may therefore be said to offer a metaphysical solution to suffering. It is really part of a trilogy of similar forms in the Exodus narrative conveying both God's power and his presence: namely Moses' staff, the Ark and the Nehushtan.

Number

> "Yea, and without these might they have fallen down with one blast, being persecuted of vengeance, and scattered abroad through the breath of thy power: but thou hast ordered all things in measure and number and weight." Wisdom of Solomon *11:20*

When considering mathematical characteristics, we must also consider the mystical meanings of numbers. This may appear unclear to those who do not comprehend the Divine Code in the physical world of our ordinary senses. The concealment of spirit underlines a much more profound mystery: the material, elemental world is destined to pass from time and become one with the Divine world we cannot yet see.

The author and occultist William S. Burroughs (1914-1997) coined the phrase the "twenty-three enigma". A curious aspect of his life was a fascination, some might say a morbid preoccupation, with numbers and particularly the number twenty-three. This came about whilst he was living in Tangiers in the early 1960s. Burroughs was introduced to a ferry captain named Clark, who boasted that he had never had a mishap in all his twenty-three years at sea. Burroughs later learned Clark had drowned in a shipping accident, and that same day claimed to have heard a radio broadcast announcing the fatal crash of flight number Twenty-Three on the New York to Miami route, which aircraft was flown by another Captain Clark. This was a synchronous trigger moment for Burroughs, who continued to experience number twenty-three phenomena for the rest of his life. Indeed, it became a motivation for his research into the occult, and he came to identify twenty-three as "the number of death". I have tried to validate Burroughs' account of the ferry sinking and "Flight-23" but without success. One tragedy I did discover was that of Atlantic Southeast Airlines Flight 2311, which crashed killing 23 people onboard, but that was in 1991. However, if we take Burroughs' story at face value, the synchronicity he encountered is certainly intriguing at the very least.

Carl Jung (1875-1961) the Swiss psychiatrist, psychoanalyst and founder of analytical psychology, identified three component elements for synchronistic events involving repeat numbers: meaningful coincidence, acausal connection, and numinosity. Burroughs' experience in Tangiers certainly ticked all three of Jung's boxes, but they were by no means unique events. Those who believe in numerology and the existence of a mathematical "code" underpinning *everything*, acknowledge that there is a positive and negative force attributed to number. If we look at Burroughs' synchronistic number twenty-three, there are observations worthy of note concerning it. The number eleven is regarded in certain gnostic Christian traditions, such as Martinism, with death. This is because it equates with the number two (11 = 1 + 1, and 1 + 1 = 2) the double energy of individuality and imbalance. The negative connotation of the numbers two or twenty (the latter by designation of the formula 20 = 2 + 0 = 2) and represent opposition, incompatibility, and negative forces. The number three represents weakness and narcissism (and numerologically is derived by the formula of 1+1+1 = 3 or 2 + 1 = 3). The combination of two or twenty and three is equated with the number five in numerology (following the numerological formula of 2 + 3 = 5, or 2 + 0 + 3 = 5). Five is a number said to represent discord and suffering.

Intriguingly, the number fifty-six (or two, by application of the formula 5 + 6 = 11, and 1 + 1 = 2) was associated by the Pythagoreans with Typhon. Typhon was the serpent deity who challenged Zeus for control of the cosmos. On his eventual defeat, the serpent was cast into the abyss. Fifty-six therefore represents duality, the suffering caused by it and the triumph of order over chaos. Fifty-six was also a geometrical label used by the eighteenth-century order of theurgists and exorcists known as the Élus Coëns[10] for the Armageddon described in the New Testament. They related it to the casting into the abyss of the Lord of Chaos, the Beast of Revelation.[11]

Patterns can be found when one looks for them, be they actual proofs of numinous occurrences or examples of apophenia (that is, "selection bias"). For instance, the World Trade Centre was attacked on 11 September 2001, and conspiracy theorists point out that in Arabic numerologically the date can be equated with the number five, thus: 1+1+0+9+2+0+0+1=14,

---

[10] Discussed in chapter 4.
[11] Revelation 20:3 - see chapter 4 of this book.

and 1+4=5. Both twenty-three and fourteen equate with the number five, both of which numbers we will explore in more detail later. So if true, the events experienced by Burroughs may be said to exemplify the negative energy identified with certain numbers in combination.

The Marquis de Sade

In his later years, the infamous Donatien Alphonse François, Marquis de Sade (1740-1814) became increasingly obsessed with numbers. De Sade was a French nobleman known for depraved sexual excess and blasphemy. However, he also wrote widely on philosophy and politics, the latter as a proponent of anarchic unrestrained free will. The numerical system de Sade was working on before he died (in a mental asylum, as it happens[12]) appears to have involved visualisation techniques focussed on the number nine, which was especially important to him.

De Sade appears to have recognised towards the end of his life that the number nine "reproduces" itself mathematically. He first noted this through the application of a numerical system, namely: $9 \times 2 = 18$ and $1 + 8 = 9$; also, $9 \times 3 = 27$ and $2 + 7 = 9$. Applying this formula, de Sade noticed that nine plus *any* digit returns to the *same* digit, thus:

---

[12] "...in August 1808 Royer-Collard, who was the chief medical officer at Charenton, took it upon himself to write to the minister of police informing him that in his opinion de Sade could not be diagnosed as mad, and that because the marquis was in the habit of indoctrinating fellow inmates with his abominable beliefs it would be best to remove him to a prison or a fortress." In D. Carter, Marquis de Sade (London, 2011) p.97.

$$9+1 = 10 \quad 1+0 = 1$$
$$9+2 = 11 \quad 1+1 = 2$$
$$9+3 = 12 \quad 1+2 = 3$$
$$9+4 = 13 \quad 1+3 = 4$$
$$9+5 = 14 \quad 1+4 = 5$$

In geometry, nine forms a circle: $360 = 3 + 6 + 0 = 9$, representing the cycle of self-generation and replenishment. However, it is also the number of excess, dissolution, and masochism - the path taken by de Sade – that did not go unnoticed by him. De Sade regarded the number as synthesising "the three worlds" of spirit, the created universe and man. He believed there is an equal and opposite effect associated with the nine principle numbers, and hence how manifestation occurs by manipulating these numerical forces, to produce a fourth world, that of effect.

De Sade concluded that the number nine symbolised completion and mastery, one aspect suggesting the transmigration of the soul. At the end of the principle numbers, nine represented return to unity and further life cycles, such as reincarnation. De Sade believed he could influence his next life through a visualisation technique that could guide his immortal soul through the nine months of human gestation. Madness, perhaps, but a belief in reincarnation and the forces of number (or a cosmic code) is a universal one. It is a theme encountered in certain other occult and esoteric schools, and even in Buddhism, which teaches that forty-nine days is the longest length of time the soul can spend in the intermediate state after death and before its rebirth, and which also happens to be seven

De Sade

weeks after conception and the point at which the pineal gland becomes visible in the human foetus.

Certain esoteric traditions identify the number five with the prevarication of Adam and his fall from grace in the Garden of Eden. The mystical meaning of the three branches of the Tree of Knowledge i.e., the pillars of judgement, balance, and mercy, were lost to man at this point. He instead became imprisoned in material matter, the flesh, deprived of his spiritual powers. This is the meaning of the well-known passage in the book of Genesis where God looks for his ashamed children:

> "And they heard the voice of the Lord God walking in the garden in the cool of the day: and Adam and his wife hid themselves from the presence of the Lord God amongst the trees of the garden." Genesis 3:8

The number five attracts special attention in the Christian esoteric tradition known as Rosicrucianism, where it symbolises the difference between humanity's first spiritual state and its present incorporation in flesh and blood. Likewise, the number nine, which is also recognised as the number of man's encampment in physical matter. Little wonder the Marquis de Sade became so obsessed with it.

> "I assumed that everything must yield to me, that the entire universe had to flatter my whims, and that I had the right to satisfy them at will." Marquis de Sade

The first four numbers represent many esoteric schools' primary or primal forces. To whatever degree they are multiplied, all numbers compute within the first ten, which in turn fall into the first four numbers, which is proved by their geometric addition to one another. These four "primordial" numbers contain all the others in them, and they are the only divine and coeternal numbers since they are the sign which represents substantially the form of man (body, soul and spirit) and the Divinity (referred to as "the Four Worlds").

Numbers, therefore, help us understand the origin of good and evil because the physical universe was created by weight, number and measure. The number one represents God, his Unity and the principle of creation; the number two is a binary of the opposites of spirit and matter (the principle of contradiction and confusion); three is the number of the triune power of thought, will and action inherent in man.

The Dance of Death, Holbein the Younger

Four is regarded as the number of the divine or spiritual faculties embodied in man, made in the image of God. His thought represents these, will, and action, the latter producing the first three faculties in a generative cycle, essentially a fourth faculty.

We may begin to appreciate that from the first ten numbers, or decad, all numbers are reducible to the first nine. Fractal mathematics, as applied in numerology, determines a pattern containing smaller and smaller versions of itself.

Dante

For example, in Dante Alighieri's *Divine Comedy*, there are repeated fractal structures, which emphasise his cosmogony. Each poem employs a decad, or 9+1=10 perspective for each of hell, purgatory and heaven, with an additional tier or portal in each that does not fully conform to the other nine layers. Thus, in Dante's *Inferno,* beyond the gateway or vestibule to hell is the first circle (limbo). The frightening inscription *Lasciate ogne speranza, voi ch'intrate* ("Abandon all hope, ye who enter here") welcomes those who pass through the gateway. This, in turn, leads to the second through fifth circles, where sinners of less heinous crimes are punished. Beyond this lies the sixth circle, or hell of heresy. Deeper still is the seventh circle, the hell of violence, which is divided into three further "rings" or

realms. The eighth circle, the hell of the fraudulent, is divided into ten further regions or *bolge,* and the ninth circle, that of treachery, is divided into four more regions. There are, therefore, nominally nine circles, but in truth, Dante's hell is divided into twenty-four spheres of nine circles plus the gateway (hence ten). The number three is therefore the fractal pattern.
Many occultists therefore regard the decad as an expression of the *value of being.* Numbers are both a sensory and at the same time intellectual sign given to humanity to distinguish different functions or values of things in both universal nature and the spirit realms. In consequence of this system of thought, all things - both spiritual and elemental - have a number assigned to them. This is the essential meaning of the "Divine Code".

Synchronicity

The Austrian psychoanalyst Sigmund Freud (1856 - 1939) founded clinical psychopathology. He was diagnosed with cancer in 1923, and in the same year, he published his seminal work entitled *The Ego and the Id*. In it, Freud argued that "multiple coincidences" with numbers are essentially a form of apophenia.[13] contributing to the formation of early delusions. Freud was particularly interested in dreamwork in the psychiatric treatment of his patients, and he developed a set of numerical "keys" for interpreting the value of

---

[13] Apophenia is the term attributed to the German neurologist and psychiatrist Klaus Conrad (1905-1961) for the experience of perceiving patterns and unmotivated connections in random or meaningless data, accompanied, in the words of Conrad by a "specific experience of an abnormal meaningfulness".

the first ten numbers, to which he attributed both positive and negative meanings. The most famous example was Freud's "Wolf-Man", Sergei Pankejeff *(1886-1979)*, a patient terrified as a child by a dream of six or seven white wolves staring in at him from a walnut tree outside his window.

In Pankejeff's painting of his dream in later life, there are five white wolves. Freud made the psychanalytical distinction between the dream in memory and the actual dream, whereby both became combined by the dreamer through his unconscious. Freud aimed to bring out the hidden meaning in the original dream by breaking down each element of the dream. For Freud, the number of the wolves appertained to a fairy tale the patient knew.

Wolves Sitting in a Tree, Sergei Pankejeff (1886-1979)

In Freudian dream-number-work, the number one signified separateness or unity; two meant opposition or harmony; three was implied the subjective or objective; four represented obstruction or clearance; five implied discord or radical change; six was incompleteness or completeness; seven was conflict or peace; eight, recurrence or infinity; nine the dissolution of the ego or progression; and zero had the same meaning as the number one. The curious part is the similarity of Freud's numerical keys with the meditative system devised by de Sade.

Carl Jung, in contrast, was interested in theories linking numbers with a natural rhythm in nature and biological mechanisms with numerical synchronistic events. Jung used these concepts to argue for the existence of the paranormal, where the symptoms of psychological or "morbid" apophenia and schizophrenia were absent. Distinguishing which were morbid, according to Jung, was a matter of pathology. Consequently, unlike Freud, he believed that the occurrence of genuine synchronistic experiences could be very real:

> "It is impossible, with our present resources, to explain ESP, or the fact of meaningful coincidence, as a phenomenon of energy. This makes an end of the causal explanation as well, for "effect" cannot be understood as anything except a phenomenon of energy. Therefore, it cannot be a question of cause and effect, but of a falling together in time, a kind of simultaneity. Because of this quality of simultaneity, I have picked on the term "synchronicity" to designate a hypothetical

> factor equal in rank to causality as a principle of explanation."[14]

F. David Peat in his study of synchronicity similarly wrote that:

> "Such experiences release considerable meaning, energy and creativity and give an intimation of the total transformation that is possible for both the individual and society. However, in so many cases people return to their lives unchanged, or with just a memory of an extraordinary experience. Only in exceptional cases does this opening of the floodgates produce a true and lasting transformation in which the self is freed from the limited order of time."[15]

In fact, the answer to Peat's observation lies in the everyday experience we have of opposing forces. We live with these influences without giving them much thought. For instance, we experience time (the passage of night and day); consciousness and unconsciousness (being awake or asleep); energy (the positive and negative flow of the electricity powering our civilisation); random chance (bad luck or good luck) and so forth. These opposing forces are particularly evident in nature; for instance the light from the Sun and the gravitational power of the Moon both play a pivotal role in the formation and sustenance of life on earth. Number therefore lies at the heart of

---

[14] C. Jung, Synchronicity: *An Acausal Connecting Principle*. (Trans. Hull, R F C, London, 1952) p. 339.
[15] Peat, F. D. Synchronicity: *The Marriage of Matter and Psyche* (Pari, 2014) p. 129.

synchronicity because it underpins the existence of everything:

> "Numerology may be regarded as the fundamental idea that numbers, mathematical symbols, quantities, measurements, and statistical analyses have yet further powers than those which display when we use them to solve mathematical problems ...numerology suggests that certain digits can affect the universe around them and can influence human behaviour, success, and failure."[16]

1913 illustration of Pythagoras and female adepts

---

[16] L & P. Fanthorpe, *Mysteries and Secrets of Numerology*, (New York, 2013), p.17.

Sacred Geometry

Geometry is the mathematical system of visualising the numerical principles of the physical universe. Pythagoras (570-495 BC) held that all things were made of numbers and, like the ancient Chinese of whom he had no knowledge, believed numbers were either masculine or feminine in character. They therefore contained the sex energy or force of the opposing principles of generation found in nature. For instance, even numbers were held to contain feminine passive energy, and odd numbers active, masculine energy. In his system, the number five therefore represented marriage and harmony, because it was the sum of the number two (the feminine principle) and the number three (the masculine principle), applying the formula: 2 + 3 = 5. To reinforce this, the Pythagoreans taught that 2 x 5 = 10, and 1 + 0 = 1, which they regarded as the "perfect number". The number one symbolised unity and God. This was therefore a very different interpretation of the number five to that taken by the Rosicrucians.

In the theory of "sacred geometry" numbers are associated with geometric forms or shapes, and these are given specific meanings. The number one for instance is symbolized by a circle. The ancient Greeks identified the serpent Ouroboros with the number one since it symbolically ate its tail to represent a repeating cycle of life. In alchemy, the ouroboros is a sigil symbolising the energy that permeates elemental matter, eternal generation and the harmony of opposing forces. It is a symbol that is found in many other ancient, unconnected cultures and civilisations.

The Aztec god Quetzalcoatl, portrayed as the Ouroboros

The number two is symbolised by two single circles overlapping one another to form the shape of a fish in the centre. This is the Vesica Piscis (which means "the Vessel of the Fish").

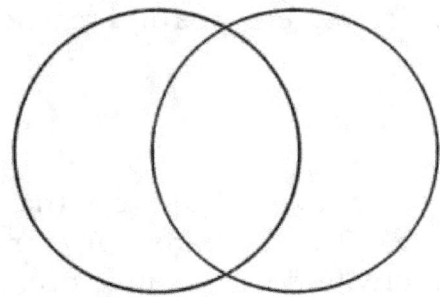

To the Pythagoreans this was the number of movement, symbolizing duality. When the two opposite forces merge their energy is greater than the sum of their individual parts, leading to the attributes of the number three. The number three is symbolized by the triangle, the perfect balancing of two opposite elements by a third mediating element. It therefore represented balance and harmony.

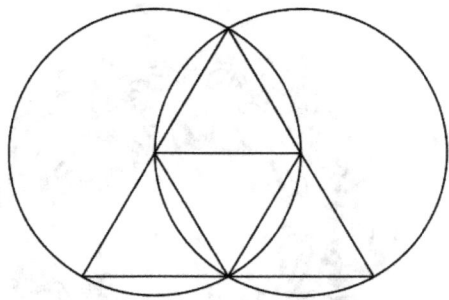

We shall consider later how the image of the Biblical Nehushtan is identified with the triangle formed in the vesica piscis of sacred geometry. This is the true meaning of the number twenty-three, the movement of dual forces (the number two) towards harmony and balance (the number three). The number four is symbolized by the square, which represents the physical world which replenishes and regenerates itself in this cycle.

The number five is symbolized by the pentagon. According to the Pythagoreans, five represented marriage or harmony and is a positive number of love.

There is, therefore, a disparity between the numerological and geometrical interpretations for the number, but which mirrors the dual aspects of nature and spirit in any event. This is explained by the fact that the number five represents the four elements of nature, plus the addition of the non-elemental substance of spirit (the fire-like material of the supernatural realms). Hence the numerological formula for five is $4 + 1 = 5$. These dual aspects for the geometric number can be represented by the positive upward pointing "white" pentagram, and the negative downward pointing "black" pentagram. Each therefore represents the influences of either good or bad spiritual forces. They also perfectly mirror one another, and emblemise the grand principle of the secret tradition, *as above, so below.*

The number six is symbolized by the hexagon. Six is both the sum and product of its factors: $1 + 2 + 3 = 6$; and $1 \times 2 \times 3 = 6$, and therefore represents correspondence, symmetry, and balance. The number seven is symbolized by the heptagon. The number seven represents perfect order, and in sacred geometry is identified with natural patters such as the days of the week, the colours of the rainbow, the seven Biblical days of creation, the musical scale and so forth. The number eight is symbolized by the octagon. When considered as the addition of seven with the number one, it symbolizes a connection to the Divine unity, infinite in natural and spiritual evolution. Finally, the number nine is symbolized by the nonagon, representing completion, mastery, and return to oneness. It is also the numerological summation of all the preceding eight numbers and geometric patterns:

- The circle has 360 degrees (3+6+0 = 9)
- The triangle = 180° (1+8+0 = 9)
- The square = 360 degree (3+6+0 = 9)
- The pentagon = 540 (5+4+0 = 9)
- The hexagon = 720 (7+2+0 = 9)
- The heptagon = 1080 (1+0+8+0 = 9)
- The octagon = 1260 (1+2+6+0 = 9)

The Twenty-Three Enigma

Returning to the theme of synchronicity for a moment (bearing in mind the numerological and geometrical interpretations given to the value of numbers as detailed above), the writer Robert Anton Wilson (a friend of William S. Burroughs) observed caustically that "when you start looking for something you tend to find it".

William S. Burroughs (1914-1997)

However, he never completely shrugged off number synchronicity as paranoid delusion or apophenia. Writing in issue 23 of *The Fortean Times*, Wilson provided examples of his own encounters:

> "As soon as I became seriously intrigued by collecting weird 23s, one of my best friends died – on 23 December. My two oldest daughters were born on 23 August and 23 February respectively. According to Omar Garrison's Tantra: The Yoga of Sex, in addition to the well-known 28-day female sex cycle, there is also a male sex cycle of 23 days. Burroughs, who tends to look at the dark side of things, sees 23 chiefly as the death number. In this connection, it is interesting that the 23rd Psalm is standard reading at funerals. Heathcote Williams,

editor of The Fanatic, met Burroughs when he (Williams) was 23 years old and living at an address with a 23 in it. When Burroughs told him, gloomily, "23 is the death number", Williams was impressed; but he was more impressed when he discovered for the first time that the building across the street from his house was a morgue." [17]

It must also be acknowledged that the number twenty-three (and corresponding "flip-side" number thirty-two) does have curious characteristics in nature:

- each parent contributes twenty-three chromosomes to a foetus (there are forty-six chromosomes in human bodies, made from twenty-three pairs);
- the average human biorhythm is twenty-three days;
- blood takes 23 seconds to circulate the body;
- the human spine is generally composed of thirty-two vertebrae; the natural number of permanent teeth is thirty-two;
- the earth's axis is tilted at twenty-three degrees;
- the ancient Chinese believed numbers conveyed sex energy, with evens representing the feminine and odds the masculine principles. They considered prime numbers to be particularly masculine and conferred a special status on the number twenty-three because it is made up of two consecutive prime numbers and the only even prime number, two;
- in the *I-Ching* the number twenty-three signifies division, and is therefore a number of generation

---

[17] *The 23 Phenomenon | RAWilsonFans.org.*

as we shall see. This may be temporary discord but it is hardly chaos, and has more to do with the eternal law of change;
- according to one Buddhist tradition, the Buddha was the twenty-third in the Earth's sphere. In the Buddhist scriptures the "Three Realms" of *Triloka* are world heaven, earth, and what lies between. The Realm of Sensuous Desire, earth, is that of material need and includes the six realms of Desire, earth and the hells;
- the Qur'an was revealed to Mohammed over twenty-three years, beginning on the twenty-third night of the 9th Islamic month;
- according to Josephus, Adam was 230 years old when Cain killed Abel;[18]
- in Jewish tradition the children of Adam and Eve numbered fifty-six. Adam had thirty-three sons and twenty-three daughters;[19]
- Aaron was 123 years old when he died;
- Jeremiah preached repentance to an obstinate people for twenty-three years;
- St. Paul refers to the killing of the twenty-three thousand idolatrous Hebrews in the wilderness;[20]
- Twenty-three is the most cited prime number in mathematics because it can only be divided by itself and the number one;
- Twenty-three is the lowest prime that consists of consecutive digits, the building block of all mathematics; and

---

[18] Josephus, *Antiquities of the Jews,* Book I ch.2, v.3.
[19] Ibid.
[20] In some translations of the Bible, it is 24,000, but in any event, Paul is confusing the killing of the 3,000 in the Golden Calf Incident with the plague of Shittim in his reference to the 23,000 deaths.

- 666 represents the Latin numeral DCLXVI, consecutive Roman numerals in descending order, which in Revelation 13:11-18 is identified as "the Beast". Intriguingly, two divided by three is 0.666.

As a lawyer, numbers have played a big part in my professional life. Yet specific numbers stand out more than they should. The numbers I experience most often are eleven and twenty-three, or fractals thereof. For instance, as an example of a never-ending pattern or "loop" for the number twenty-three, the number five figures prominently, too. My daughter was born on the fifth day, at 5:55 PM, in room five, and moved to ward five of the local maternity hospital. After many years of curious and inexplicable coincidences, I began to keep a record like Robert Anton Wilson. The following events are entries from *a few days* in my life a couple of years ago. They range from the mundane to more surreal events:

- driving down a country lane I seldom used on my way to work, a cyclist pulled into the road without looking. I narrowly avoided him and, as I passed, noticed he had the number "twenty-three" printed on the back of his shirt;
- upon arriving at work I switched on my computer to see twenty-three unopened emails;
- my first meeting that morning was with an elderly client, but she had collapsed in a nearby shop. Her friend came into my office to explain the situation, stating "I've been her close friend for twenty-three years";

- a new client came in to see me. His date of birth was twenty-three November and he lived in house number eleven;
- a client rang shortly afterwards in a state of distress, telling me her bank thought she was deceased and had frozen her account. She was advised by them that she had to wait twenty-three days to get it sorted out;
- I popped out of the office to grab a bite to eat for lunch. I passed a man wearing a tee-shirt loudly stating "New York Sinner Twenty-Three";
- I randomly looked up an eBay item I was selling, and it came up as having twenty-three hours left to sell;
- my wife texted me to say she had been looking at a display of garden centre merchandise and sent me a picture of house numbers (the kind you put on the front door). What stood out was not the number twenty-three in the picture, but the fact it was upside down in unopened packaging, and had been placed out of numerical order next to the number eleven;
- my son's new iPhone – he had only had it a few days – suddenly developed a fault and stopped charging at twenty-three percent;
- a client called because the copy of her will had not arrived in the post. It transpired the Post Office had sent it to the wrong house number – number twenty-three;
- using my satnav to plan a journey the following day, it stated an estimated arrival time of 11:23 and the journey would take 23.3 miles;
- I received an enquiry from a colleague's client about a will – it was dated the twenty-third;

- a new client's address was 23 High Street. Her driver's licence was issued on May 23rd and she referred me to a letter that a rival law firm had sent her dated the twenty-third;
- there was a misplaced codicil at work dated the twenty-third;
- I was shown to a restaurant table by a server at lunch: she led me to table number twenty three;
- I experienced a tyre blow-out on my way home from work. It happened approaching exit twenty-three. Opening the boot of the car and removing the doughnut for the first time, the number twenty-three had been written in chalk beneath it;
- I booked a couple of seats at the movies to watch a picture with my wife. The tickets were for Row H seats sixteen and seventeen in the centre. Upon arriving, we moved along row H looking for our allocated seats. Next to seat fifteen was the number 23. The sequence of seating then continued at number seventeen. There was no explanation for this.

It will be recalled that these events took place over a period of just *few days*. Another curious experience occurred when my wife and I were staying overnight at a friend's unoccupied house, when there was a sudden and unexplained thumping on the drawing room wall and, upon entering, a digital clock was flashing 23:23. Another instance of note took place when we were recently on vacation in Rome. For the flight we had been reassigned to seats twenty-two and twenty-three on row something-or-other, and our boarding gate had been changed to gate twenty-three. During our stay in the city, we visited the Colosseum. The arches at ground level were numbered by the Romans as they had a sophisticated ticketing system, but we were unaware of this at the time. As we walked past the Colosseum, my cell 'phone rang and I took a call from my father telling me our home had been burgled. The date was the twenty-third, and when I ended the call, I looked up saw that we had stopped right under portico numbered XXIII. Of course, poor old Julius Caesar was also stabbed twenty-three times in Rome, I forgot to mention that.

It may strike you that many (although not all) of these synchronicities were negative and occasionally downright distressing. Indeed, my experiences of the number twenty-three generally are. It associates itself with difficulty for some reason. However, experiences of discord, like those encountered by Burroughs and Anton Wilson, are *not* entirely random since they appear to follow some form of natural law - however understood. This observation is key to what follows later. For present purposes, it is sufficient to note that numbers represent a code built into the fabric of our material universe, much like gravity and time.

Chaos

For the Israelites aimlessly looping around the Sinai for forty years, suffering was experienced in decay and physical privation. This is an allegory of spirit encamped in time and material space. These negative experiences corresponded with the hope of entering the land of Canaan and the intermediate assistance they received in the form of the miracles performed in the wilderness. This encounter of opposing forces results in the transformation of nature (through conscious thought) and becomes the progenitor of eternal, incorruptible life. How so? If Egypt represents the fallen state of man in captivity to nature, then the wilderness is the intermediate stage of spiritual evolution and ascent leading to heaven, represented by the land of Canaan. We will recall that in the natural world, each parent joins to create a third person, a brand-new life. We may also recollect elementary school physics, wherein as children we were taught that electricity is created by the interaction of opposites (both positive and negative) clashing to create energy. In very simple terms movement leads to effect, and the movement of Israel from Egypt to Canaan is an allegory of redemption.

To put all of this all into context, our thoughts and actions are essentially forces, out of which something arises. In the far eastern religions the effect or outcome is known as karma, the original meaning of which simply meant "deeds." In karmic terms, each of our acts results in good or bad results, suffering or pleasure depending on what deeds have taken place. It is also a fact that innocent people can be caught up in collective karma, such as a disaster, terrorism or war.

The Brazen Serpent is a symbol of the generative power of opposing forces, or types. The story of the Nehushtan begins with the Hebrew people bemoaning their lack of comfort. They cannot all have complained, but those that did felt that slavery in Egypt was preferable to wandering around in hunger.

These people were angry at God. In this instance, the choice of slavery versus freedom, and despair versus hope were met by thoughts and actions that were negative, and the outcome of which was a plague of venomous snakes on everyone as God's protection was withdrawn from the collective. Men often risk forgetting the spiritual beings they are, and that from which they have been separated. The deadly bites of the serpents may be an allegory for the insinuations of demons on the thoughts, will and actions of the people. Within the context of the Biblical narrative, the Hebrews undertook new crimes which required the operation of a measure of justice in response, so as to clearly establish the law of God in their minds. The pain of the body, soul and mind in this punishment corresponded with the corrupted spiritual faculties inherent in the victims.

The Siege of Jerusalem, 13 July 587 BC

There is, however, another interesting link, and one that fits well with the Egyptian faith system familiar to the Hebrews. This is the giant snake or serpent god, Apep, the Lord of Chaos and spirit of evil. The third century BC funerary spells known to us as the Coffin Texts recite how Apep was born from the Sun god Ra's umbilical cord and used his evil eye to hypnotise him. Apep attacked the spirit of the living and the dead alike at night with an army of demons.[21]

The Egyptians would endeavour to dispel the evil of Apep by destroying his effigy. Thus, if the Israelites equated the attacks of the fiery seraphim with Apep and his hordes, then the Brazen Serpent may have been perceived as a talismanic form of counter or sympathetic magic made in his image. However, we are still left with the fact that the Nehushtan was laid up in the Jerusalem Temple and not destroyed until many centuries later by Hezekiah.

Symbols of chaos can be found in many cultural and divinatory contexts. A. E. Waite (1857-1942) identified the Tower in the classic Ryder-Waite Tarot deck as "a card of confusion" reminiscent of the destruction of the Jerusalem Temple.[22] Waite understood the card to represent the triumph of evil in the material world and the catastrophe of the "fall" of spirit into a material state and animal form. Papus (Gérard Encausse (1865-1916) renamed The Tower "the Lightning-struck Tower" and believed that it signified the fifth element of the spiritual world "incarnated" (encamped) in the visible and material world. He also wrote that the card

---

[21] Cited from Ancient Egypt Online: Apep (Apophis) at ancientegyptonline.co.uk.
[22] Ibid. The Pictorial Key to the Tarot.

represented the material fall of Adam into four-fold elemental matter.

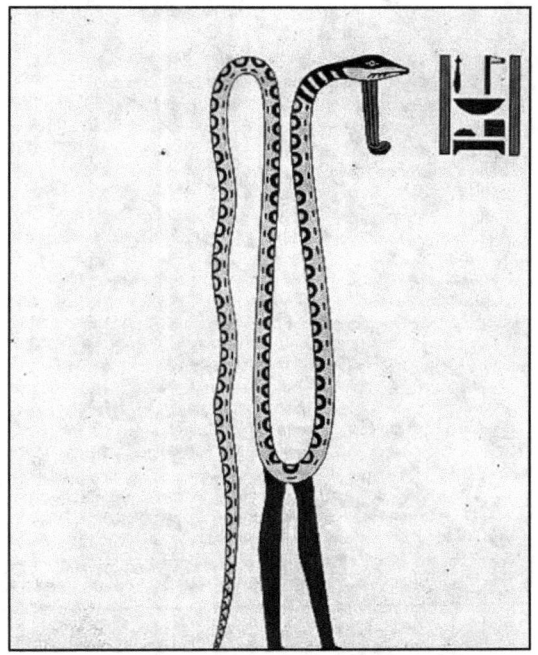

British Museum (author's photograph)

Papus' designation of the card is not entirely negative, however, as he believed it also represented the "materialization" of the redeeming Holy Spirit into the visible world of chaos. In any event, it appears to configure to a card of the encampment of the spirit (the fifth element) within the four natural elements of air, fire, water and earth, and the debasement of spirit into the realm of organic chaos and destruction.

The flip side of course is that God becomes present in our realm of Malkuth, the lowest sephira in the Kabbalistic Tree of Life. Interestingly, the lightning strike on the card bears resemblance to the shape and venomous strike of a serpent, which mirrors the role of the snake in the myth of the fall of Adam and Eve.

In many ways, the image of The Tower card is reminiscent of the Nehushtan as an icon of God's Spirit, or Presence, locked in the material matter of its composition – wood and metal – each representing the dual elements of moveable and fixed matter, earth and fire. The latter represents the Divine substance of spirit, and the former the material earth. Suppose we see this image as two constituent parts that interlock.

In that case, we can perhaps draw an analogy with the Seal of Solomon too, since it is the convergence or 'meeting' of the Divine with the spirit of man, which the following classical alchemical image of the ouroboros illustrates.

> "On him ...we have permission ... to demand from the angels of destruction that they take a sword to this wicked man... to kill him ... for handing over the Land of Israel to our enemies, the sons of Ishmael." *Pulsa Denura* ("Lashes of Fire")

The *Pulsa Denura* is an ancient Aramaic ritual which purports to inflict death on its victim within a year. The source for the ritual is to be found in the Jewish theurgical rites the *Sefer HaRazim* and the *Sword of*

Moses.[23] The *Sword of Moses* is an apocryphal book of magic dating from around the first century AD, which begins with a description of the heavenly realms and angels, and provides various invocations and theurgic procedures to be able to manipulate the fate of others. The Aramaic word pulsa means "attack" and *denura* is "fire". The *Pulsa Denura* is therefore an *attack of fire* by invocation, and one which by tradition requires at least ten exponents to perform (reminiscent of the ten angels who brought plague on Egypt). The attack of the fiery seraphim on the Hebrews' camp is also suggestive, perhaps, of a curse, and one which appears to have been a misuse of the same attack on Adam and Eve in the Garden of Eden. The Sword of Moses contains invocations such as the following:

> "If at a full moon you wish to seize and to bind a man and a woman so that they will be with each other, and to annul spirits and blast-demons and satans, and to bind a boat, and to free a man from prison, and for everything, write on a red plate from TWBR TSBR until H' BŠMHT. And if you wish to destroy high mountains and to pass (in safety) through the sea and the land, and to go down into fire and come up, and to remove kings, and to cause an optical illusion, and to stop up a mouth, and to converse with the dead, and to kill the living, and to bring down and raise up and adjure angels to abide by you, and to learn all the secrets of the world, write on a silver plate, and put in it a root of

---

[23] G. W Dennis, *The Encyclopaedia of Jewish Myth, Magic and Mysticism*: (Second Edition, London, 2016).

artemisia, from TWBR TSBR until H'BŠMHT. For a spirit that moves in the body, write on magzab from TWBR until MNGYNWN. For a spirit that causes inflammation, write from MGNYNWN until HYDRST."[24] The Sword of Moses

God restored his dispensation to facilitate the rehabilitation of the Hebrews – once justice was satisfied. He ordered Moses to make the bronze image of a fiery serpent and to raise it high on a pole, which is suggestive that the Nehushtan may possibly have been a totem of sympathetic magic used by Moses in response to the *Pulsa Denura*.

Once it was lifted up, the people looked at it and they were instantly protected from the attack. The image is one of opposites: the fiery serpent of burning bronze and the pole symbolising the magical staff or wand of Moses. It is, above all else, a symbol of God's power over life and death. In numerological terms, the opposing forces or pillars of death and life, the number two (1+1=2), are harmonised into one emblem understood by the number three (2+1=3), representing the power of God over life and death through his Thought, Will and Action. The three "spiritual "faculties of man are also thought, will, and action, and it is in this sense that we are made "in the image of God"

---

[24] Y. Harari, *The Sword of Moses (Ḥarba de-Moshe): A New Translation and Introduction* in *Magic, Ritual, and Witchcraft* (University of Pennsylvania Press, Volume 7, Number 1, Summer 2012) pp. 58-98.

Moses in Judgement on the People, by Hans Holbein the Younger

It is also possible that the "fiery-serpents" were bolts of lightning striking the Hebrews' camp. Strikes of lightening reflect the shape of serpents, and intriguingly the Aztec fire serpent Xiuhcoatl was represented by a serpentine bolt of lightning, because he was spirit in the form of the fire deity. In Mesoamerican mythology lightning was a weapon borne by the gods against their enemies in the underworld. Xiuhcoatl therefore symbolized the forces of darkness being driven out by the fiery rays of the sun.

Thunder and lightning played a large role in Greek mythology too. Zeus, the god of lightning and justice, was able to harness it as a weapon of justice to hurl at the unfaithful. In the rabbinical writings of the twelfth century, the sound of thunder is likened to the sound of God moving, and is a precursor of the manifestation of the Divine Presence.

British Museum (author's photograph)

Unsurprisingly, in the book of Exodus there is an instance of a lightning strike amongst the people, announcing the direct contact of the Hebrews with God at the foot of Mount Horeb:

> "And it came to pass on the third day in the morning, that there were thunders and lightnings, and a thick cloud upon the mount, and the voice of the trumpet exceeding loud; so that all the people that was in the camp trembled. And Moses brought forth the people out of the camp to meet with God; and they stood at the nether

part of the mount. And mount Sinai was altogether a smoke because the Lord descended upon it in fire: and the smoke thereof ascended as the smoke of a furnace, and the whole mount quaked greatly. And when the voice of the trumpet sounded long, and waxed louder and louder, Moses spake, and God answered him by a voice." Exodus 19:16-19

The implication is that the Nehushtan reflects sympathetic magic. However, the bronze seraph is not used apotropaically to destroy evil, but to heal its victims. This is possibly because, in the Biblical narrative, the plague was brought about by the conduct of the people.

In much the same way as the "serpentine" lightning strikes augured the appearance of Divinity, so the fiery serpents preceded the appearance of the Nehushtan. Divine justice was rigorous, yet it was only aimed at the reconciliation of men with truth. In the Old Testament, mercy always accompanies effort. There is no manifestation of justice that does not serve as an example of this truth. God having been satisfied, made known to the people the sweetness of consolation and who, by this sudden contrast, learned to know the difference between the spiritual and the demonic life. Above all else, the Nehushtan reminded them that God's power was always superior to that of his enemies.

It follows that, when the people looked upon the Nehushtan, they knew something which is no longer immediately apparent to us today: namely, that which appeared as one object was multiple objects imbued with supernatural qualities. The Hebrews were aware that they stood in the presence of God, as if standing in a symbolic Garden of Eden, where the Tree of Life and the Tree of Knowledge of Good and Evil stood side by side, two forms in three aspects. The Zohar ("The Book of Splendour") is a set of twenty-three books forming a Jewish esoteric and allegorical commentary on the Torah, most likely dating from around the eleventh century AD, or later. The meaning given to the Nehushtan in the Zohar is that, by looking at the Brazen Serpent, the people were reminded of why they deserved punishment, which became the first step toward their repentance and forgiveness.[25] The Zohar goes on to say that thought is as indivisible as the mind that produces it; it is also the principle of every free spiritual act, and the greatest of the three spiritual faculties mentioned earlier. Thought may therefore be equated with the number one, because it engenders will, without which all thoughts cannot produce anything. The will, by its binary rank with the number one, is perceived as the number two, but it also *proceeds* from thought and represents the number three.

However, thoughts and intentions are of no effect if they are not implemented. This action, by its ternary rank, is also equal to the number three, and by adding to it the preceding ternary of thought and the will of which proceeds from it, completes the number six, which correspondingly represents the active number of the days of the creation. The Mishnah tells us that looking at the Brazen Serpent was not what cured the

---

[25] The Zohar, Sh'lach Lecha, verse 175.

Israelites. Instead, it was the act of *looking up to God* that cured them.[26] Looking up to God resembles the four elements pointing upwards towards the Divine, who in turn reaches downwards. This mirrors the duality of the masculine, animating forces (air and fire) and the feminine, or passive, forces (water and earth).

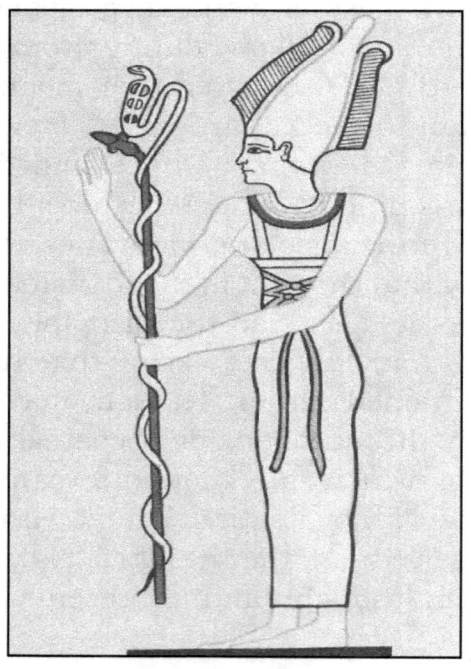

British Museum (author's photograph)

We see that by looking at the Nehushtan, the power of thought and will (2) is put into action (3). These forces are matched by the power of God's threefold faculties, with the result that the creative forces immediately heal the afflicted. There is, therefore, a mathematical or numerical code behind miracles. The geometric form

---

[26] Mishnah *Rosh HaShanah* 3:8

for this numerical code is the Seal of Solomon, the Star of David, representing the threefold faculties of both God and man in conjunction with one another:

2 | Nehushtan

The caduceus is a symbol of two snakes intertwining around a herald's staff. In antiquity, this was associated with the Greek god Hermes, the *kēryx* or messenger of the gods, and protector of travellers. In association with Mercury, the patron deity of the alchemists, Hermes carried the serpentine caduceus or herald's staff.

The *kēryx* was not originally equated with Hermes, but with the athletic messengers delivering diplomatic communications between the Greek city states, known as the *kerykes*. The antecedence of this association may be much older, given that the caduceus derives from ancient Samaria, where the serpent deity known as *Ningishzida* ("the Lord of the Good Tree") was worshipped from around the fourth century BC, coincidentally (?) at the beginning of the Bronze Age.

The name Ningishzida has a curious etymological similarity with the word "Nehushtan" and its connection with food provision (Ningishzida was the Samarian god of agriculture). The symbol of Ningishzida was a staff with two intertwined snakes. The god's staff was understood to hold the power of life and death. The composition of the Biblical Nehushtan alludes to the metallurgical processes of smelting and the magical powers represented by Moses' staff. One serpent is made of burning bronze affixed to a pole; the other is a living seraph immanent within (a representation of the Tree of Life). This implies that Like the Nehushtan, the caduceus symbolised the active and passive forces in creation, the bringing together of the material and the spiritual into one form, and its subsequent effect on nature. It is an image expressing the duality of temporal and spiritual power

Quetzalcoatl, British Museum (author's photograph)

operating on one another. Double-headed or paired serpents are also an enduring theme in Mesoamerican mythology and religion. In the Aztec language, *coatl* means serpent or "twin" and forms part of the name of important deities such as Quetzalcoatl and Coatlicue, the gods who represented the axis between the centre of the earth and heaven.

Curiously, this perception of the double-headed serpent appears in Egyptian religion too, and can be seen here on papyri illustrating the barque of Ra with a prow and stern figurehead of serpents, carrying the soul of the deceased Pharaoh between the tomb on earth and the celestial realms every day and night.

British Museum (author's photograph)

The image below is an Aztec ceremonial mask in the British Museum, showing a pair of serpents entwined around the eyes, nose and mouth, representing the sensory attributes of a synthesis of the rain god Tlaloc and the creator god, Quetzalcoatl.

British Museum (author's photograph)

In the Pentateuch, the absence of balance invariably leads Israel into death and suffering, until harmony is restored. In the plague of the fiery serpents, we see discord and disruption. The remedy is reconciliation with God by the harmonisation of this dissonance, which is only achieved through transformation. This, of course, is the sole objective of the *Magnum Opus* (Great Work) of alchemy. It is no coincidence that in ancient Egypt it was believed the dead were judged in a "Weighing of the Heart" ceremony. This is commonly misunderstood to refer to moral conduct, but in truth it is about the balance of the personality-soul.

The plague of fiery serpents was not imposed by God for capricious reasons, any more than the ten plagues afflicting Egypt. True, the Bible describes God "hardening" Pharaoh's heart, but this is simply another way of describing the barrier or envelope influencing Pharoah's thoughts. In any event, this action was required to separate the Hebrews from the Egyptian gods which Pharoah represented in his claim to be an incarnate divinity. In a sense it was a bout of god-versus-god, and the rules were therefore different. It also explains why Moses' original demand was only for the people to be allowed to worship in the wilderness. Suffering was the result as the consequence of this barrier or falling away from God. Nonetheless, the sufferings of Egypt had a corresponding act of mercy by God once the Hebrews departed: since he left the Egyptians alone. We see a correspondence of this in the plague of fiery serpents afflicting the Hebrews, when Moses pleads to God to restore his dispensation once the envelope or barrier of their ingratitude and lack of faith is removed.

Our encampment in material form is the chief source of human suffering. This is because the physical universe is subject to the law of time, and therefore entropy. Chaos and death are simply part and parcel of our existence here. The Hebrews' act of volition or compliance to the will of God by looking at the Nehushtan had the effect of healing, and to that extent, the brazen serpent and pole represented a bridge or portal between the material cosmos and the heavenly realm. If we recall that numbers and geometric forms are mathematical codes and images for the cosmos, then the Nehushtan symbolically embodies these. This makes even more sense if we regard the corresponding aspect of the Nehushtan as a representation of the Mind of God.

Why serpent symbolism? The obvious answer lies in the fact that the venomous snakes attacking the Hebrews were associated with avenging Egyptian magic, and that serpent worship was commonplace at that time (in both its positive as well as negative aspects, as we have seen). Nonetheless, in many Biblical narratives there are often tantalizing hints at historicity which challenge solely allegorical interpretations. The fact that the serpents are described as "fiery" is revealing, because there is an extremely venomous species of cobra native to Egypt known as the Red Spitting Cobra. It is, as the name suggests, red, and is a nocturnal animal whose venom contains a lethal mixture of cytotoxin and neurotoxin which it literally spits into the eyes of its victims. At face value, the Nehushtan equates to a form of antivenom, albeit quite unlike modern antitoxins which are chemically produced from the infected immune systems of donor animals. That said, in ancient Egypt serpents symbolised the essential life force *(ka)* of the kingdom and were also regarded as having both healing and destructive powers. Regarding the latter, it is conceivable that some form of antivenom may have existed in antiquity but, regardless, the Red Spitting Cobra would have attacked anyone unfamiliar with the topography of Egypt who happened to stumble across its path in the dark.

Hezekiah

2 Kings 18.4 brings the Nehushtan into connection with the Brazen Serpent of Numbers 21:9, where we discover that at some point in antiquity it had been laid up in the Jerusalem Temple complex. In that politically unstable period, the Nehushtan was deemed to be a rival to the authority of the secular and religious authorities, and was eventually removed and apparently destroyed by King Hezekiah of Judah (739-687 BC), the thirteenth king of Judah, who witnessed the destruction of the northern Kingdom of Israel by the Assyrians . To improve Judah's ailing fortunes, he ordered massive religious reform, including the prohibition of venerating "foreign" deities.

> "He trusted in the Lord God of Israel; so that after him was none like him among all the kings of Judah, nor any that were before him." 2 Kings 18:5.

> "[Hezekiah] broke into pieces the bronze serpent that Moses had set up on a standard, for the Israelites had been offering idolatrous sacrifices to it. It was called Nehushtan." 2 Kings 18:4

the Nehushtan's placement in the Temple, bearing in mind the serpent-worship commonplace in the Middle East of the period, was most likely because it was by then something of a money-spinner. The priests would have sold ketoret to its worshippers, an expensive incense for exclusive use at the Temple:

> "Take unto yourself sweet spices, stacte, and onycha, and galbanum; these sweet spices with pure frankincense: of each shall there be a like weight: And you shall make it a perfume, a confection after the art of the apothecary, tempered together [salted], pure and holy: And you shall beat some of it very small, and put of it before the testimony in the tabernacle of the congregation, where I will meet with you: it shall be unto you most holy. And as for the perfume which you shall make, you shall not make to yourselves according to the composition thereof: it shall be unto you holy for the Lord. Whosoever shall make like unto it, to enjoy the smell thereof, shall even be cut off from his people." Exodus 30:34-38; 37:29.

If we consider the causes of iconoclasm of any kind, the reason behind the practice is usually political. In this instance the threat came from the shift of Judah away from the uraei or serpent worshipping Egyptians to the more powerful Assyrians, whom Hezekiah's father had opposed militarily in support of Egypt. When Egypt was soundly thrashed in battle by the Assyrians in 701 BC, the Assyrian king Sennacherib agreed to peace with Hezekiah in exchange for money. In 2 Kings 18:14-15 we read that Hezekiah paid Sennacherib "...vessels of copper, iron, bronze and tin...". So, there was clearly a metal-grab taking place in Jerusalem, and the bronze component of the Nehushtan probably vanished into the royal mint.

Nevertheless - and particularly in the Book of Deuteronomy - there is a recurring impulse to break or destroy images for religious reasons too. Hezekiah did not begin his reforms, if such they were, by destroying the Nehushtan. He first broke the stone pillars or sacred stone posts known as the Asherah poles, which were wooden poles that once stood near the altars in Canaanite sacred places.

Asherah was the mother goddess or feminine divinity worshipped by the Canaanites. The Asherah poles in Judah therefore probably symbolised some form of fertility cult. However, Asherah is also identified with the Egyptian deity Qetesh, the deity who oversaw the expulsion of foreigners from Egypt during the intermediary period. This was approximately at the time of the Exodus. Coincidence? The Talmud records that, by the time of Hezekiah, the Nehushtan had come to be viewed as an object of idolatry, a type of snake-god, since snake worship was widespread.

This leads us to consider why Hezekiah wanted to remove the stone pillars of the Canaanite Asherah poles and destroy the Nehushtan in the first place. We have seen that there was a political dimension, namely that he had to pay-off the Assyrians, and the Nehushtan was bronze and had monetary value. The removal and melting down of valuable resources were an outcome of losing the war. Yet, the Nehushtan may also have resembled the pagan Asherah poles that Hezekiah disliked. Indeed, there is every probability the pole itself was a sacred rod from Canaanite times. Neither of these connotations would have been popular by the time of Hezekiah's reign, which was in a state of national emergency.

The Peddler, Hans Holbein the Younger

We learn that the people had taken to burning incense to the Nehushtan and worshipped it for salvation. Its original purpose appears to have been all but been forgotten. What was not lost on the religious reformers of that period, however, was that the Nehushtan, represented serpent dominance by way of an idol. No doubt it may still have been held to cure those who believed ("looked upon it"), since its integral purpose was to effect salvation through a serpent under the threat of serpents.

Order

> "In the middle of the journey of our life I found myself within a dark wood where the straightway was lost." Dante, *Inferno*

In the Gospel of John, the adept Nicodemus sneaks out under cover of dark to hold a conversation with Jesus on the Mount of Olives. Today the Church of All Nations, built over the rock on which Christ is believed to have prayed before his betrayal, stands beside what remains of the ancient olive tree ghettos which once covered the entire hill. A fence of iron tracery guards the gnarled trunks of the few remaining trees, of considerable age and said to have been there for some 2,000 years because they replenish themselves. Here, amid these living symbols of eternal life, the Pharisee Nicodemus - a member of the Sanhedrin – would seek answers from Christ. The Jerusalem Sanhedrin was an assembly of twenty-three elders, appointed to sit as a criminal court.[27] It is this same Nicodemus who argues a point of jurisprudence in Jesus' favour following his arrest, and who appears after his crucifixion to provide embalming spices for his burial (John 19:39). Nicodemus is troubled in his soul. During this exchange, Jesus identified himself with the Nehushtan.

---

[27] Interestingly, Tola one of the Judges of Israel, judged Israel for 23 years (Judges 10:1-2).

> "And as Moses lifted up the serpent in the wilderness, even so must the Son of man be lifted up." John 3:14

In so doing, Jesus would have been imparting a clear message to the Sanhedrin via Nicodemus. On a superficial level the passage in John prefigures the crucifixion. The analogy was such that any learned teacher of Israel would have understood in clearly Messianic terms. This is because the Brazen Serpent represented the burning bush, and to stand before it was to be in the very presence of God. It will be recalled that the pole upon which the brazen serpent was raised also symbolised the Tree of Life.

The meeting took place on a raised position overlooking the Jerusalem Temple. When Jesus associates himself with the Nehushtan, he is making a direct parallel with Moses standing before the burning bush, and is essentially telling Nicodemus that he is the Tree of Life (which was believed to have stood on the Temple Mount, the location of the Garden of Eden overlooked by the Mount of Olives).

> "And I believe I have hit upon the reason why our Master used this figure, and talked to Nicodemus with metaphor after metaphor, and figure after figure, because the root of all language must be in figures." Charles Haddon Spurgeon

Just as the living serpent, wand, pole and Brazen Serpent were united, so the human and divine natures of the Messiah were harmonised in the Incarnation, since Christ is both fully God and fully human. It is in foretelling his being raised upon the cross, or tree, that Christ makes the analogy between himself and the Nehushtan, reassuring Nicodemus that he will heal and protect the people who "look upon" him with faith. In this sense the Nehushtan is a direct precursor to the cross. This theme of duality is firmly mirrored in the Gospel account, since Nicodemus approaches Jesus at night, alluding to suffering in the dark night of the soul, unsure of faith and struggling to understand God. Nicodemus had listened to Jesus in the Temple forecourt earlier in the day, and now reaches out to him, but in private and under cover of darkness. Metaphorically he cannot see or look upon Jesus clearly at all. Nicodemus knows Israel has been enveloped in a barrier of ignorance and ingratitude, and which has estranged it from God. He addresses Jesus as "Rabbi" (teacher), a mark of respect and acknowledges him as such, "for no man can do these miracles that thou doest, except God be with you." (John 3:2) Jesus replies with one of the most cryptic and difficult responses in the Gospels: "Except a man be born again, he cannot see the kingdom of God." (John 3:3)

Nicodemus is stupefied, but Jesus adds another obscure response by adding: "Except a man be born of water and of spirit he cannot enter into the kingdom of heaven." (John 3:5). There is a good deal to be drawn from these few words which cast a light on Nicodemus' dilemma, and indeed that on the plight of the covenanted people. Firstly, Christ speaks of first "seeing" before "entering" the kingdom of heaven.

These are two quite different things, and one cannot be achieved without the other, but only in due order. Likewise, he refers to both a mystical or spiritual rebirth in terms of the unification or harmonisation of water and spirit. There are many levels of understanding regarding these words, but essentially in the alchemical tradition "spirit" is symbolically equated with elemental fire, and to be born of both water and fire means to harmonise the mind (the "elemental vapour" of water) with the Divine Fire or Substance that is the essence of Divinity. A substance like fiery water makes no sense in the physical world and cannot be described by reference to the material senses, but in the spirit realm they are one and the same. Water when heated by fire becomes vaporous and forms a cloud. Jesus is alluding to the pillar of cloud and pillar of fire, by which God manifested 1 Kings 7:15 states the Boaz and Jachin were made of *nehoshet*, a pure copper or bronze. Yet, in truth, there is only one pillar, albeit there *appear* to be two:

> "And the angel of God, which went before the camp of Israel, removed and went behind them; and the pillar of the cloud went from before their face, and stood behind them: and it came between the camp of the Egyptians and the camp of Israel; and it was a cloud and darkness to them, but it gave light by night to these: so that the one came not near the other all the night." Exodus 14:19-20

Whilst presented as opposites, the pillars have a unity of substance and represent the divine, fiery substance of the one, living God. If Nicodemus had at any time been a High Priest, then he would have entered the Holy of Holies on the Day of Atonement to find it empty, and the *shekinah* or Spirit of God absent. Nicodemus appears to have similarly returned disappointed after meeting Jesus on the Mount of Olives, or perhaps at best left disheartened. On reflection, he may have come to understand how the column of fire guiding his soul by night shifts it position to become the column of water providing its protection by day. In between these columns is the middle path he is to follow, in recognising Jesus as the foretold Messiah. The rebirth of which Jesus spoke is the recognition in the adept of what lies beyond the physical senses, in the spiritual realm, which follows its own laws. However, it also represents a change in the way of perceiving things on earth too.

> "That which is born of flesh is flesh; and that which is born of the Spirit is spirit." John 3:6

There is symbiosis with the apostle Paul's first-hand account of being "born again", and of seeing (but not entering) "the third heaven" as we shall see in the following chapter. Nicodemus, languishing in darkness, suffered as a direct consequence of his ignorance, much as the Hebrews did in the wilderness. So, we can begin to see that Jesus was trying to tell him to look upon him as if to look upon the Nehushtan, and to be healed and reconciled with God. Nicodemus had a choice. He could remain locked in the physical sensory realm of perception and suffer in it; or he could choose to transform the non-physical part of himself (his mind, that which was born of both fire and water) to perceive God and to reintegrate with him. Nicodemus intuitively knows there is more beyond the physical senses, hence he would not have made his way in the middle of the night to ask. Jesus' words, at least initially, were ciphers to him, and no doubt brutally challenged his ego: "Art thou a master of Israel, and knowest not these things?" John 3:10

I would be very surprised if Christ did not say these words with a twinkle in his eyes, seeing the supreme irony of it. Approaching Jesus, Nicodemus was seeking light. Nicodemus is an allegory of course for a 'type' of person who has acquired status and exoteric knowledge, but who does not have much self-knowledge. He was seeking an allegorical 'antivenom' from the forces supressing his progress in that regard. He was given a formula by Jesus, who told him straight: "we speak that we do know and testify that we have seen and ye receive not our witness." In other words, Nicodemus had to re-boot his way of perceiving things if he was to stand any chance of escaping his dark night:

> "This night which, as we say is contemplation, produces in spiritual persons two kinds of darkness or purgation, corresponding to the two parts of man's nature – namely, the sensual and the spiritual. And thus the one night or purgation will be sensual, wherein the soul is purged according to sense, which is subdued to the spirit; and the other is a night or purgation which is spiritual, wherein the soul is purged and stripped according to the spirit, and subdued and made ready for the union of love with God."[28] St. John of the Cross (1542 – 1591)

Let us consider again the sequence of Jesus' words in John chapter 3:

---

[28] St John of the Cross, *Dark Night of the Soul* (Trans. P. E Allison, New York, 2003) pp. 19-20.

- no one can see the kingdom of God unless they are born again;
- no one can enter the kingdom of God unless they are born of water and the Spirit;
- flesh gives birth to flesh, but the Spirit gives birth to spirit;
- the wind blows wherever it pleases. You hear its sound, but you cannot tell where it comes from or where it is going. So, it is with everyone born of the Spirit;
- no one has ever gone into heaven except the one who came from heaven—the Son of Man;
- just as Moses lifted the snake in the wilderness, so the Son of Man must be lifted up, that everyone who believes may have eternal life in him; and
- whoever believes in him is not condemned, but whoever does not believe stands condemned already because they have not believed in the name of God's one and only Son.

There are strong alchemical references in these seven oblique sayings. Mystical as they are, the sequence establishes a recombination of the primary elements into the three essentials of fire and air (the soul), air and water (the spirit), and earth and water (the body). This is the meaning of being born again of water and the spirit. Everyone who dies believing in the healing power of Christ (as in the Brazen Serpent) can avoid rebirth in the flesh and be born of the spirit (the fifth element of alchemy) and attain immortality upon entering Heaven. In the same way, as God did not immediately remove the fiery serpents from among his people, so he has not removed the consequences of man's (Adam's) original sin. Christ is explaining that, like Adam, we must suffer sorrow and hardship in our encampment in the four elements of the flesh. Still, in death, the soul escapes this physical reality and commences the initial stage of alchemical transformation (when we shall "see" heaven on our journey towards "entering" it). This is the real meaning of being raised. In Genesis, God promised that the seed of woman would crush the serpent's head ("and I will put enmity between thee and the woman, and between thy seed and her seed; it shall bruise thy head, and thou shalt bruise his heel" Genesis 3:15), and just as Moses lifted up the Brazen Serpent so shall all who look in faith upon the incarnate Christ, in who's humanity he is the woman's seed ("the Son of Man"). There can be little doubt that the writer of the Gospel of John is setting out an alchemical formula for the divinity of Christ incarnate, and his identification within the Nehushtan is central to this vision.

It may be recalled that Nicodemus had earlier witnessed the Cleansing of the Temple, when Jesus had attacked the tables of the money changers, in a fashion mirroring the divine wrath of the plague of fiery serpents upon an adulterous and ungodly people. He appears to have understood that this was "a sign" or announcement of the punishment that would soon overcome the nation. The Messiah was not only a redeeming figure but was also understood to be the manifestation of justice among the covenanted people. At this moment, the people were attacked in the spirit because they were overcome by materialism, which was contrary to their intended destination. For this reason, they did not recognize the Liberator that Nicodemus had a sense of:

"And when he had made a scourge of small cords, he drove them all out of the temple, and the sheep, and the oxen; and poured out the changers' money, and overthrew the tables; And said unto them that sold doves, 'Take these things hence; make not my Father's house an house of merchandise.' And his disciples remembered that it was written, 'The zeal of thine house hath eaten me up.' Then answered the Jews and said unto him, 'What sign shewest thou unto us, seeing that thou doest these things?'

"Jesus answered and said unto them, 'Destroy this temple, and in three days I will raise it up.' Then said the Jews, 'Forty and six years was this temple in building, and wilt thou rear it up in three days?' But he spake of the temple of his body. When therefore he was risen from the dead, his disciples remembered that he had said this unto them; and they believed the scripture, and the word which Jesus had said."
John 2:13-22

Our experiences in life compel us to recognise the existence of two opposed principles of good and evil. That which allures us to each, compels us to experience the manifestation of either. For this reason, Louis-Claude de Saint-Martin stated that we must accurately understand and gain knowledge of our present condition; that is, 'to know thyself.' To quote Saint-Martin: "We are far nearer to that which we term the other world than to this" (*Des Erreurs et de la Verite*).

We can only commence our first steps towards reintegration in conformity with God's will. In occupied East Jerusalem, one of the most striking churches in the city, the Church of St Peter in Galicantu, commemorates Peter's denial of Christ. Under the present church there is a cell thought to be where Jesus was detained for the night following his arrest. In those days it was in total darkness. Without light, Christ had been lowered through a carved, deep hole in the floor. It can only have been a place of utter desolation, terror and torment. The dungeon is an earthly version of the place we might call Hell, a place of darkness and malevolence. Whether Christ was ever there we do not know. It is tradition.

Punished in the spirit, the Jews of the Diaspora were deprived of their Temple and place of true worship. This culminated a sequence of prevarications that ultimately led them into a new exile. In the Messianic Age that came to be, man was to learn to metaphorically collect up the rubble of the ruined Temple and carefully rebuild it within himself. In the end, if the individual does not take advantage of sharing this metaphorical "Promised Land" he has no hope of avoiding the terrible despair of which Christ spoke to his disciples. To "look upon" Christ is therefore analogous to looking upon the Nehushtan in the wilderness, the mediator that Job cried out for, but who ultimately was the universal Nehushtan for all people:

> "For he is not a man, as I am, that I should answer him, and we should come together in judgement. Neither is there any daysman betwixt us, that might lay his hand upon us both." Job 9:32

Centuries after its destruction, the Nehushtan was still remembered in the folk memory of the Jewish people as a powerful symbol of grace. It symbolised the twin pillars of justice and mercy being brought into balance by the Divine Mind behind the intimacy of the Spirit of God's revelation and the unfathomable Divinity. To know the Spirit is to know God, and vice versa. The effect of this merging of knowledge and understanding is the transformation of our mind and its integration into our personality, precisely what Nicodemus had sought.

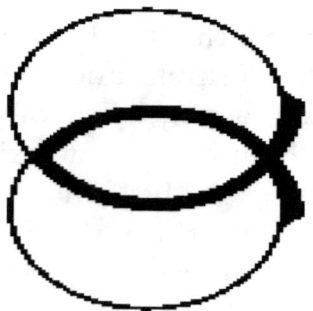

In sacred geometry, this is represented by the form of the *vesica piscis* (symbolising the number two) and the triangle immanent within it (symbolising the number three). In a sense, it mirrors the overlapping Seal of Solomon. The ichthus[29] symbol in which the geometric triangle appears, was adopted by early Christianity

---

[29] The Greek word for fish

and consists of two intersecting arcs, the ends of the right side extending beyond the meeting point to resemble a fish. In the centre of the overlapping circles, the two opposite forms converge to become a third form. The form it produces cannot, of course, exist independently of the two overlapping forms.

Job and His Friends, Gustave Doré Bible

In the Rosicrucian myth of Adam Kadmon (the primordial or first human being, with whom Christ identifies himself as "the Son of Man"), we encounter the story of a spiritual being who enjoyed the same virtues and powers as the hierarchies of angels. Adam Kadmon's role was to hold judgment over the fallen angels, the demonic fiery seraphs. In St. Paul's Damascene conversion, the apostle briefly became "as one" with the Mind of Christ in his "near death experience", when the light blinds him and falls off his horse. Following this episode, and upon his recovery, the apostle reacquired some of Adam Kadmon's original powers. This echoes the powers given to Moses at the burning bush, when he came within sight of God and stood in his presence. There are many instances in Paul's ministry of miraculous, supernatural powers being demonstrated, but one of the most intriguing is the story of the twelve Ephesian men empowered by the apostle to speak "in the tongues of angels."

> "And it came to pass, that, while Apollos was at Corinth, Paul having passed through the upper coasts came to Ephesus: and finding certain disciples, he said unto them, 'Have ye received the Holy Ghost since ye believed?' And they said unto him, 'We have not so much as heard whether there be any Holy Ghost.' And he said unto them, 'Unto what then were ye baptized?' And they said, 'Unto John's baptism.' Then said Paul, 'John verily baptized with the baptism of repentance, saying unto the people, that they should believe on him which should come after him, that is, on Christ Jesus.' When they heard

this, they were baptized in the name of the Lord Jesus. And when Paul had laid his hands upon them, the Holy Ghost came on them; and they spake with tongues and prophesied. And all the men were about twelve." Acts 19:1-7

While material processes on earth cannot destroy the indwelling presence of the Divinity (the Spirit), it can nonetheless lay dormant and suppressed. The supernatural powers conferred on Paul are a reminder of hope amid suffering and his story, like that of Nicodemus, is that of man seeking out God, and God seeking out man. Once again, this is nothing less than a glimpse of the path of return to the original state man enjoyed before Adam Kadmon's fall from grace, and encampment in the physical form of flesh.

Alchemy

In alchemy, serpent symbolism is represented by the metallic element of mercury, the *serpens mercurii*, understood by the alchemists as the opposing regenerating force of life, death, and immortality. The alchemists used serpent symbolism to awaken the human mind to the realities concealed by the physical senses, by recalling the soul to knowledge of its original, spiritual memory. It is in this context that the serpent encountered by Adam and Eve in the Garden of Eden did not equate with Satan and the personification of evil, as the Church teaches. The Garden Serpent represented man's desire and ego and brought about destructive change. The root meaning of the Hebrew word for serpent, as we have seen, is *nahash,* but it can also mean intuitive knowledge and natural ability. It describes humanity's innate capacity to captain its own soul and evolve. However, the Hebrew noun *nehoshet* (meaning copper or bronze) also carries an alternative negative interpretation: that of promiscuity. These words, therefore, have dual meanings, much like the name and application of the Tree of Knowledge of Good and Evil. The fiery serpents in the book of Numbers are, therefore, the consequence of ingratitude, disloyalty, and pride.

Adam and Eve, Emile Bernard, early 20th century, ink On Paper

The caduceus of the Graeco-Egyptian deity known as Hermes Trismegistus (an amalgamation of the Greek messenger-god Hermes and Thoth, the Egyptian god of knowledge) was a staff entwined by two winged serpents. According to ancient mythology, Hermes' staff originally belonged to the blind Theban prophet Tiresias, who stumbled upon two snakes reproducing. He promptly took it upon himself to kill one of them with the staff he was carrying to prevent their increase. Tiresias dispatched the female snake first and was promptly transmuted into a human woman until he could locate and kill the corresponding male snake, seven years later. Another myth has it that Tiresias separated two fighting (not mating) snakes with his wand, and by so doing brought about peace. The story of the Nehushtan fits quite comfortably into this mythology, as with other ancient serpent symbolism. Again, we see powerful dual forces being either removed or harmonised. Numerologically, these are represented by the number two, which has the negative aspect of unresolved conflict and harmful consequences. However, it also has the positive potentiality of balance, especially if that third force – the outcome of thought and will – is constructive.

The "Burning Ones" of the Old Testament were winged celestial beings identified with the angels. A basic etymology of the word leads us to a possible connection with the Egyptian god Serapis, the serpent god of protection. The cult of Serapis had its origins in the worship of Wadjet (meaning "seat of the eye"), and the Hebrews may have identified the Nehushtan with Wadjet, a deity connected initially with Osiris and the Apis bull. Apis was believed to have taken the form of a bull on earth and was perceived as a symbol of salvation:

> "And when the people saw that Moses delayed to come down out of the mount, the people gathered themselves together unto Aaron, and said unto him, Up, make us gods, which shall go before us; for as for this Moses, the man that brought us up out of the land of Egypt, we know not what is become of him. And Aaron said unto them, Break off the golden earrings, which are in the ears of your wives, of your sons, and of your daughters, and bring them unto me. And all the people brake off the golden earrings which were in their ears and brought them unto Aaron. And he received them at their hand, and fashioned it with a graving tool, after he had made it a molten calf: and they said, These be thy gods, O Israel, which brought thee up out of the land of Egypt." Exodus 32:1-4

The Incident of the Golden Calf reminds us that the raising of the Brazen Serpent was neither an isolated occurrence, nor one that was entirely divorced from the religion of ancient Egypt. When Moses descends from Mount Horeb with the first, complete tablets of the Law, he arrives to find the people worshipping the Golden Calf. Moses is incensed by the idolatry and smashes the tablets upon it and arranged to place them within the Ark of the Covenant, along with Aaron's serpent-staff. The early Hebrews may have believed God to be the Creator of the universe, but they did not deny the existence of lesser gods or the spiritual hierarchies. Indeed, the generally negative connotations with which serpents are treated in the Bible belies the fact that they had a positive treatment in other near and far eastern religions. For instance, the Indian Vedas describe the *Nagas*, a syncretic blend of both human and reptilian beings, as celestial beings bringing kundalini energy. In the apocryphal books of Enoch,[30] the serpent Gadrel seduced Eve and introduced humans to weaponry[31] (another form of protection). This alludes to the Enochian myth relating to the creation of the human-angel hybrids known as the Nephilim, the "giants" engendered when the "Watchers" fell to earth and reproduced with human women. Yet, the seraphim also performed a positive role. Enoch tells us that the seraphim are called "the Fiery Ones" because they burned the scrolls on which Satan, the emissary of God, recorded sin:

> "Why is their name called seraphim? Because they burn the tablets of Satan. Every day Satan sits with Samma'el, Prince of Rome, and with Dubbi'el, Prince of Persia, and they write down the sins of Israel on tablets and give them to the seraphim to bring them before the Holy One, blessed be he, so that he should destroy Israel from the world." 3 Enoch 35:12

In this text, some of the seraphim exercise free will to act as intermediaries and protectors of the people. We

---

[30] The books of Enoch were written in the intertestamental period of 200 BC to AD 200.

may therefore begin to appreciate the more positive context in which the Nehushtan was originally understood, and conversely why Hezekiah's reforms were directed at routing out vestiges of syncretised religious beliefs.

There is also the myth of the two "Enochian Pillars". Josephus records a tradition that the descendants of Seth, the third son of Adam, sought to prevent the loss of true knowledge in the diluvian flood by erecting two pillars:

> " ... one of brick and the other of stone, and inscribed these discoveries on both; so that, if the pillar of brick disappeared in the deluge, that of stone would remain to teach men what was graven thereon and to inform them that they had also erected one of brick."
> 1 Enoch 68:6-7

The reinvention of writing was credited to the Samarian scribes who discovered it on the surviving stone pillar. While the pole of the Nehushtan is most likely wooden, there is also a tradition of the pillar of brick being made of wood. The pole on which the Nehushtan was affixed may be symbolic of wisdom or knowledge, which makes perfect sense if "looking up to" it is a cure for the stricken, since knowledge of healing counts among the chief wisdoms. In this sense the raised serpent alludes to the reconciliation of man and nature with God.

3 | **Dunamis**

> *"By his power God raised the Lord from the dead, and he will raise us also." 1 Corinthians 6:14*

Saul of Tarsus (AD c. 5 – c. 64) was at the forefront of the violent persecution of the nascent Church. In Galatians we are told he was "advancing in Judaism beyond many his own age" (Galatians 1:13–14). In Acts we read that he was "thoroughly trained" in the Pharisaic school of Gamaliel, and "was zealous for God." His enthusiasm and proximity to the Pharisees enabled him to "take the coats" of the men who stoned Stephen to death:

> "And when the blood of your martyr Stephen was shed, I stood there giving my approval and guarding the clothes of those who were killing him." Acts 22:20

To guard the clothes of those stoning heretics was a particularly high honour, conferred on officials of the High Priest:

> "And that is just what I did in Jerusalem. On the authority of the chief priests, I put many of the Lord's people in prison, and when they

were put to death, I cast my vote against them." Acts 26:10

The death of St. Stephen, Woodcut at Lambeth Palace

Yet it was while Saul was "breathing out murderous threats against the Lord's disciples" (Acts 9:1) that something unexpected, terrifying and powerful happened to him. Paul tells us that this transformation was not the consequence of any human involvement:

> "I received it by revelation from Jesus Christ. For you have heard of my previous way of life

in Judaism, how intensely I persecuted the Church of God and tried to destroy it. ...But when God, who set me apart from my mother's womb and called me by his grace, was pleased to reveal his Son in me so that I might preach him among the Gentiles, my immediate response was not to consult any human being." Galatians 1:11-16

Saul's epiphany, as described in Acts, saw him travelling from Jerusalem to Damascus with a warrant from the High Priest[32] to commence an inquisition there. His journey was halted by "a blinding light" from heaven "that flashed" around him, accompanied by a sound and the voice of Jesus exclaiming "Saul, Saul, why do you persecute me?" (Acts 9:4). It is worth recalling here the description of the descent of the Holy Spirit on the twelve Apostles in Acts, which resembles and perhaps describes a similar occurrence:

> "Suddenly a sound like the blowing of a violent wind came from heaven and filled the whole house where they were sitting. They saw what seemed to be tongues of fire that separated and came to rest on each of them." Acts 2: 2-3

The inquisitors accompanying Saul heard "the sound" but did not see anything (Acts 9:7). Later in Acts we read that these companions did not hear anything either, and it is interesting to note that the Greek verb for voice or sound (*akousia*) is also translatable as "understanding." Saul's

---

[32] Josephus records that it was Jonathan, the son of Annas who the officiating high priest.

companions therefore did not understand the phenomenon they had witnessed. The psychological connection had not been made, whereas for Saul it had. Saul was led into Damascus, where he remained blind for three days, unable to eat or drink (Acts 9:9). His blindness is allegorical of death, and mirrors Jonah's three days and three nights in the belly of the whale and Christ's three days in Hell (1 Peter 3:18).[33]

St. Paul, Martin Schongauer, c.1480

---

[33] Matthew 12:38-41, Romans 10:7, and Ephesians 4:7-10 refer to Christ's descent into Hell.

Paul later described his experience in a letter to the Corinthian church:

> "I know a man in Christ who fourteen years ago was caught up to the third heaven—whether in the body or out of the body I do not know; God knows. And I know that such a man—whether in the body or out of the body I do not know; God knows—was caught up into Paradise and heard things that are not to be told, that no mortal is permitted to repeat." 2 Cor. 2:12

Ananias is called by God in a vision to go to the house where Saul is laid up, to explain what has happened and to restore his sight. Ananias is fearful of his persecutor, but the same voice commands him: "Go, Saul is my chosen instrument." Ananias places his hands on Saul, and immediately "something like scales" fall from his eyes. This may of course have occurred, but equally it may be allegorical of Saul's *gnosis* or awakening. From that point on, the new man "Paul" acquired some of the Adamic powers wielded by man before the Fall:

> "The signs of an apostle were wrought among you in all patience, in *signs*, and wonders, and mighty deeds" 2 Cor 12:12

What were these "signs" and "mighty deeds", and how was Paul able to perform them? What had happened to him, and in what sense does it connect to the Divine Code contained within the Nehushtan? It is clear the gifts (powers) exercised by Paul were transformative and restorative powers given for the purpose of *demonstrating* faith. For the former Pharisee "thoroughly trained in the Law of his ancestors", it was now the resurrected Christ who was the fulfilment of Divine revelation, demonstrable to men through a threefold confluence of signs (*sermion*), wonders (*teras*), and mighty deeds (*dunamis*). As we read in 1 Corinthians:

> "My message and my preaching were not with wise and persuasive words, but with a demonstration of the Spirit's power, so that your faith might not rest on human wisdom, but on God's power." 1 Corinthians 2: 4-5

The Greek word *dunamis* was more commonly used in Paul's time to convey a sense of explosive force, or energy.[34] The description in Acts of the descent of the Spirit in the Apostles and the Damascene experience provide a tantalizing glimpse of the force empowering these chosen initiates. It is a power which shapes Paul's understanding of his transmutation from death to life, figuratively applied to all those justified through faith in the redemptive death and resurrection of Christ, the fully reintegrated Second Adam (the Middle Pillar of the Temple connecting man and God). It follows that Paul's conversion was a terrifying event, akin to what we might today describe as a 'near death experience.' It was a restoration from death to life, with immense transformative implications for Paul:

> "I want to know Christ – yes, to know the power of his resurrection and participation

---

[34] The modern English word dynamite derives from it.

in his sufferings, becoming like him in his death." Philippians 3:10

In Paul's writings there is an explicit connection to raising the dead in his description of this force or energy. In Acts we have a detailed description of the Apostle physically lying on top of a deceased body, placing his arms around it, and giving a demonstration of the "wonder" and "sign" of restoring life before a large crowd of eyewitnesses:

> "And there were many lights in the upper chamber, where they were gathered together. And there sat in a window a certain young man named Eutychus, being fallen into a deep sleep: and as Paul was long preaching, he sunk down with sleep, and fell down from the third loft, and was taken up dead. And Paul went down, and fell on him, and embracing him said, Trouble not yourselves; for his life is in him. When he therefore was come up again, and had broken bread, and eaten, and talked a long while, even till break of day, so he departed. And they brought the young man alive and were not a little comforted." Acts 20:8-12

Eutychus' body is broken and smashed by his fall, the cause of his death. Yet he is completely restored to full health by Paul. The word for 'wonder' used by Paul (teras) is more accurately translated as *sudden shock* or *terror*.[35] Such

---

[35] Paul describes examples of the signs of the Spirit: "To each one the manifestation of the Spirit is given for the common good. To one there is given through the Spirit a message of wisdom, to another a message of

demonstrations (*apodexi*) of the Spirit would have been shocking to the numerous onlookers.

The raising of Eutychus from a 19th century illustrated Bible

For instance, in Acts we read of Paul's prison gate being mysteriously unlocked and opened (Acts 12:10); of a "cloud of darkness" blinding a rival magus;[36] a

---

knowledge by means of the same Spirit, to another faith by the same Spirit, to another gifts of healing by that one Spirit, to another miraculous powers, to another prophecy, to another distinguishing between spirits, to another speaking in different kinds of tongues, and to still another the interpretation of tongues." (1 Cor.12: 5-10).

[36] Elymas also known as Bar-Jesus. Acts 13:6. The name.'*Elymas*' is possibly derived from the Arabic *alīm* for 'learned" or 'wise' (Acts 13:11-12).

transfer of power received from his apron (Acts 19:11-12); the casting out of demonic spirits (Acts 16:18); and an earthquake powerful enough to break the chains of his prison wall and tear off the door (Acts 16:26). In Acts 19:6 we read of twelve men being empowered by him to speak in tongues, that is, receiving a transfer of *gnosis*.

Paul refers to the test the convert must face of passing through the transmutative power of God:

> "Now concerning spiritual gifts, brethren, I would not have you ignorant. Ye know that ye were Gentiles, carried away unto these dumb idols, even as ye were led. Wherefore I give you to understand, that no man speaking by the Spirit of God calleth Jesus accursed: and that no man can say that Jesus is the Lord, but by the Holy Ghost. Now there are diversities of gifts, but the same Spirit. And there are differences of administrations, but the same Lord. And there are diversities of operations, but it is the same God which worketh all in all. But the manifestation of the Spirit is given to every man to profit withal. For to one is given by the Spirit the word of wisdom; to another the word of knowledge by the same Spirit; to another faith by the same Spirit; to another the gifts of healing by the same Spirit; to another the working of miracles; to another prophecy; to another discerning of spirits; to another divers kinds of tongues; to another the interpretation of tongues: But all these

worketh that one and the self-same Spirit, dividing to every man severally as he will. For as the body is one, and hath many members, and all the members of that one body, being many, are one body: so also, is Christ. For by one Spirit are we all baptized into one body, whether we be Jews or Gentiles, whether we be bond or free; and have been all made to drink into one Spirit. For the body is not one member, but many." 1 Corinthians 12:1-20

It was time for initiates to discover Christ through the transformative power of the Spirit:

"Know ye not that ye are the temple of God, and that the Spirit of God dwelleth in you?"
1 Corinthians 3:16

It is the Spirit that raised Christ to be at the Father's side in the Third Heaven. It is likewise through the Spirit that Christ communicates his will on earth. It is this which connects the immortal spirit in man to God's Spirit. Through his training with Gamaliel in Jerusalem, Paul was familiar with the doctrine of the Spirit as an emanation, or manifestation, from God. It was the Spirit that hovered over the formless void at creation and, as the harmonisation of the dual nature of God, engendered the complimentary halves of man. It is the Mirror of Jehovah, the Great Architect of Worlds. The Spirit walked alongside the First Adam; wrestled with Abraham and spoke to Moses from the burning bush. For Paul, the glory of the Spirit is manifest in creation, concealed, and revealed in all. Paul alludes to this union with the Spirit when he describes the resurrection body:

"Our bodies are buried in brokenness, but they will be raised in glory. They are buried in weakness, but they will be raised in strength. They are buried as natural human bodies, but they will be raised as spiritual bodies. For just as there are natural bodies, there are also spiritual bodies." (1 Cor. 15:43-44)

Beyond Death

What of course we see here – and what connects all of this with the Nehushtan – is elemental matter being transmuted into the spirit imprisoned within it since Adam's fall from grace. This transformation of the fixed and moveable elements of earth, water, air and fire into the *prima materia* of the ether (or 'stuff') of the spirit is the true goal and course of alchemy. The duration of our sufferings on this plane are determined by the length of our encampment in elemental nature. Just as the Hebrews "looked" upon the Nehushtan to be healed from the snares of the fiery serpents, so too does "looking" upon the cross in faith offer hope in the form of the promise of restoration and liberation from death. The *dunamis* or power enjoyed by Adam was that of a spiritual being in direct communion with God, for whom there was no need of an intermediary, and whose mission was the reconciliation of the fiery seraphs with God. Both the Nehushtan and the cross symbolise this process of restoration, and both impart knowledge of those powers over the primal chaos of creation. Those "with the Spirit" who are able to "look" upon the Brazen Serpent and the cross alike, acquire judgement. In the cosmogony of St. Paul, this equates to having "the mind of Christ." He acknowledges the intimacy of the Spirit with the unfathomable mind of God, and therein lies the power innate in the Divine Code. To know the spirit encamped within nature is to know God.

This reminds us of the original emanated man in the Rosicrucian tradition, who as we shall see, was given judgement over the fallen angels. Like Adam, Paul was at one with the Mind of Christ, the indwelling presence of Divinity which cannot be destroyed by any material processes on earth. The supernatural powers conferred on Paul were a powerful reminder of hope in Christ amid suffering, which is what we see in the emblematic Nehushtan. Ultimately, Paul's story like that of the Hebrews in the wilderness, is the mystery of man's connection to God. In *The Lazarus Effect*, Dr Sam Parnia, founder of the Human Consciousness Project, states that:

> "The goal in medicine is generally cure. Medicine is often in the pathophysiology of disease, though not for the sake of it but as a means of identifying the opposite, which is the cure"[37]

Parnia goes on to say:

> " ... that entity we define as consciousness, the soul, or the self - that which makes me who I am – does not stop existing just because someone has entered the period

---
[37] S. Parnia, *The Lazarus Effect* (London 2013) p.292.

beyond death ... if the mind – consciousness (or soul) – can continue to exist and function when the brain does not function after death, then it raises the possibility that it may be a separate undiscovered scientific entity that is not produced through the brain's usual or electrical processes"[38]

The research of the Russian thanatologist Konstantin Korotkov[39] on the phenomenon of electrical coronal discharges ("kirlian energy fields") provides an interesting correlation with some of the resurrection stories in the New Testament. Korotkov was granted permission to analyse cadavers delivered to Moscow hospitals one to five hours after physical death. The bodies of the deceased were observed by volunteers for several days. Korotkov noted the "smooth" and rapid deterioration of bodily decomposition. However, he also monitored the continuance of gaseous "energy discharges" with each type of body (looking at different genders, ages, and the range of deaths, accidental, suicidal, violent, unexpected, natural etc.). Korotkov's experiments proved that these energy flows were unconnected to physical decomposition and indeed, was the energy identified as Kirlian. These discharges followed set characteristics with some variation depending on the manner of death, and age of the victim etc. Typically, the energy flows peaked at midnight and again at three AM over three days, then stopped. Among Korotkov's observations was a numinous sense of being watched during the peak energy flow periods, as if in the presence of a living person. Science does not

---

[38] Ibid.
[39] K. Korotkov, *Light After Life* (St. Petersburg, 2014).

yet understand the processes that take place after death, or indeed at what point life is said to end. Indeed, Christ's tarrying four days to raise Lazarus, what took place at the Resurrection, or even St. Paul's raising of Eutychus, may be about the confluence of powers to raise physical bodies to life at the right time. The Nehushtan is a part of this continuum-mythology.

British Museum (author's photograph)

True, the Nehushtan did not restore the dead to physical life, but to look upon it certainly saved them from death, contrary to the opposing forces contained in the Ark of the Covenant, which instantly killed the profane foolish enough to touch it. The Brazen Serpent, therefore, "marks" (with the sign of the tau?) those who are to be saved. What Parnia describes as the "consciousness, the soul, or the self" in the immortal mind of man does not cease to exist at physical death; this reminds us that the Nehushtan myth also refers to consciousness and spiritual death, not just physical. If the will and thought of man is so estranged from the will of God that our fall into elemental matter deepens to such an extent that belief in the existence of the spirit ceases altogether, then this would almost certainly be a second death: the dead end or cul-de-sac of atheism, with its gloomy promise of non-existence following the death of the physical body. This may be the allegorical meaning of the material desires of the Hebrews at Edom when they are fixated solely on food and a return to slavery in exchange for it. However, perhaps salvation from this kind of death is averted by faith in God and trusting in him, such that looking up to the raised Brazen Serpent reconnects the mind to the existence of spirit and the Divine will. This then would be spiritual salvation and life, over which the snares of the fallen demonic entities (or banal materialism) exert no influence. In this sense, the Nehushtan also prefigures the Messiah, who came not to deliver humanity from physical death but to offer immortal life in the spirit.

Therefore, the raising of the Nehushtan is a statement of God's power over death, in much the same way as Paul's "raising" of Eutychus from physical death, and of the mastery of Divinity over both the natural and spiritual realms. To emphasise the point, there are several passages in the New Testament describing the "Harrowing of Hell" by Christ after his death and prior to his physical resurrection. These are descriptions of God's power over material death and the spiritual realms, as they take effect in the intermediate state:

- "now that he ascended, what is it but that he also descended first into the lower parts of the earth." (Ephesians 4:9)
- "whom God hath raised up, having loosed the pains of death: because it was not possible that he should be holden of it." (Acts 2:24)
- "by which also he went and preached unto the spirits in prison." (1 Peter 3:9)
- "and having spoiled principalities and powers, he made a shew of them openly, triumphing over them in it." (Colossians 2:15)

Likewise, the miracles of Jesus demonstrate God's power over the material plane. Two miracles stand out for me in particular: the curing of the woman suffering a discharge of blood for twelve years, and the story of the raising of Jairus' twelve-year-old daughter. The events take place consecutively within the same narrative in the Gospel of Mark. The text is worth reciting in full, since it brings together several themes that we have been discussing thus far; namely the intention or mental projection of man (demonstrated by "looking up" in faith; and the downwards power of God's rule over life and death). It is this power which is demonstrated in the manifestation of Divine Thought, Will and Action in elemental, physical matter:

> "And, behold, there cometh one of the rulers of the synagogue, Jairus by name; and when he saw him, he fell at his feet, and besought him greatly, saying, 'My little daughter lieth at the point of death: I pray thee, come and lay thy hands on her, that she may be healed; and she shall live.' And Jesus went with him; and much people followed him,

and thronged him. And a certain woman, which had an issue of blood for twelve years, and had suffered many things of many physicians, and had spent all that she had, and was nothing bettered, but rather grew worse. When she had heard of Jesus, she came in the press behind, and touched his garment. For she said, 'If I may touch but his clothes, I shall be whole.' And straightway the fountain of her blood was dried up; and she felt in her body that she was healed of that plague. And Jesus, immediately knowing in himself that virtue had gone out of him, turned him about in the press, and said, 'Who touched my clothes?' And his disciples said unto him, 'Thou seest the multitude thronging thee, and sayest thou, Who touched me?' And he looked round about to see her that had done this thing. But the woman fearing and trembling, knowing what was done in her, came and fell down before him, and told him all the truth. And he said unto her, 'Daughter, thy faith hath made thee whole; go in peace and be whole of thy plague.'

"While he yet spake, there came from the ruler of the synagogue's house certain which said, 'Thy daughter is dead: why troublest thou the Master any further?' As soon as Jesus heard the word that was spoken, he saith unto the ruler of the synagogue, 'Be not afraid, only believe.' And he suffered no man to follow him, save Peter, and James, and

John the brother of James. And he cometh to the house of the ruler of the synagogue, and seeth the tumult, and them that wept and wailed greatly. And when he was come in, he saith unto them, 'Why make ye this ado, and weep? The damsel is not dead, but sleepeth.' And they laughed him to scorn. But when he had put them all out, he taketh the father and the mother of the damsel, and them that were with him, and entereth in where the damsel was lying. And he took the damsel by the hand, and said unto her, 'Talitha cumi'; which is, being interpreted, 'Damsel, I say unto thee, arise.' And straightway the damsel arose, and walked; for she was of the age of twelve years. And they were astonished with a great astonishment. And he charged them straitly that no man should know it; and commanded that something should be given her to eat." (Mark 5:22-43)

The narrative in Mark immediately follows the exorcism at Gerasa, and appears in all three of the Synoptic Gospels. The stories are combined, and the link appears to be the number twelve, being the connection between the twelve years of suffering of the woman and the age of Jairus' daughter. *Prima facie* this is a narrative comparing the stricken woman's faith and the distraught father's test of faith. The number twelve is the key theme linking this combined narrative's significance. If we recall that in numerology there are ten primary numbers, then the meaning of twelve in this context is that of 1+2=3. There are in fact three events: the exorcism at Gerasa, the healing of the woman and the raising of the dead child. The number three does not derive its principal power from itself, but operates instead on the direction of forms in both the celestial and terrestrial spheres.[40] Three is the number of the mercurial-terrestrial number of the solid part of bodies, in correspondence with the fiery element of the soul, the immortal part of man.[41] The conclusion is that Christ operates the celestial or spiritual *dunamis* (power) on the material world through an act of will, and in all three episodes, those who are seeking help look up to him in faith.

In the ancient Egyptian Weighing of the Heart Ceremony, the god Osiris judged the dead by weighing their hearts against a feather or reed. If the heart was heavier than the feather then the dead were denied access to the Field of Reeds, and their heart would be eaten by Ammit (the divinity in the form of a man with a crocodile's head). The heart in ancient Egypt was the seat of the soul, and so it was not a physical human organ of which the myth speaks, but the form of the soul itself, comprised at it is of that weightless, fiery fifth element of spirit. In this sense physical death is but the beginning of the journey of transmutation, since the soul loses its physical form and must decamp to the higher realms where the path of reintegration continues. Let us think of the Nehushtan in purely symbolical terms and regard the fiery serpents as an allegory of death.

---

[40] Op.Cit. Waite. p. 404.
[41] Ibid. p. 404.

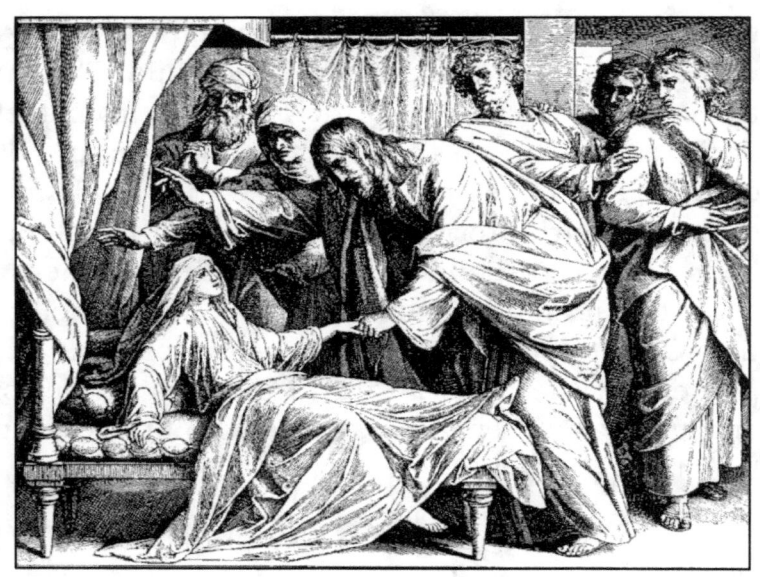

The raising of Jairus' daughter by W.B. Conkey

The power of the Raised Serpent over death is that of a metaphorical resurrection and rebirth. Physical death remains, but the hope of eternal life in the spirit remains by looking upon it. In his book *Heaven and Hell*, Emanuel Swedenborg (1688-1772) would write:

> "When someone's body can no longer perform its functions in the natural world in response to the thoughts and affections of its spirit, then we say that the individual has died. This happens when the lung's breathing and the heart's systolic motion have ceased. The person, though, has not died at all. We are only separated from the

physical nature that was useful to us in this world. The essential person is still alive."[42]

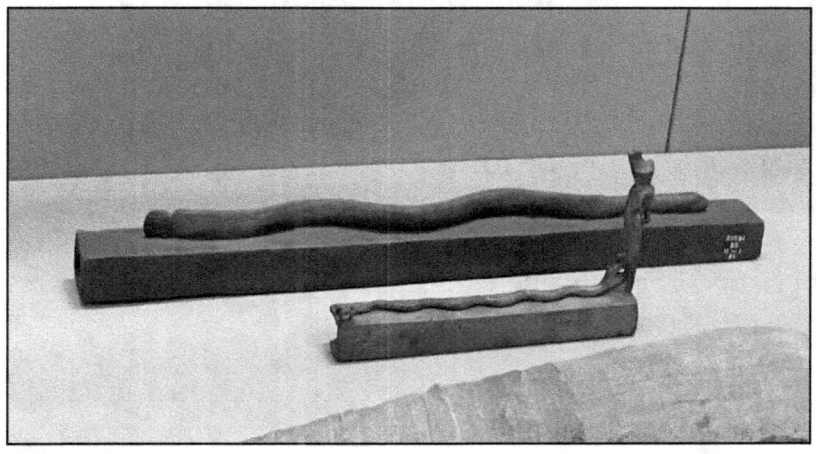

Mummified snake. British Museum (author's photograph)

The Greenback

Hopefully you are now able to appreciate how the "Divine Code" manifested in the form of the Nehushtan, as a symbol of the power of God. In a sense, it represented the will of God and of the Hebrews' collective will responding to Divine Thought, as communicated in God's directions to Moses. It might be said that if the will is the sum of personality, then death or finality sets it apart from the Divine Will. The Nehushtan was an icon of death and symbolical resurrection, the serpent and the Tree of Life combined as a unity. The distinction between subject and object had melted away, so that there was no longer any distinction between the thinker and that which was

---

[42] E. Swedenborg, *Heaven and its Wonders and Hell* (Trans. J.C. Ager, West Chester, 2009).

thought upon looking at it. This is a form of Divine union, and the reason why looking upon the Nehushtan had such a powerful effect on the consciousness of the Hebrews. This intimacy and oneness with God was found in the binary generation of thought and will creating an effect by "looking upon" the symbol. In her beautiful book *The Secret Code: the mysterious formula that rules art, nature and science*,[43] Priya Hemenway explains the existence of this "Divine Proportion" or balance existing in nature, architecture, the arts, science and mathematics:

> "Using the language of comparison and mathematical relationships we apply the Divine Proportion to life's mysteries by placing the larger next to the smaller and holding them both up to the whole. What we discover is a relationship of balance, harmony, and symmetry that is quite uncanny; and it is as mysterious in its functioning as the code we seek to break."[44]

For all that, the ancient symbol of the caduceus became a recognized symbol of that ultimate use of number by man: money. The caduceus is a representation of the ouroboros serpent, a symbol for eternal renewal. The symbol has conveyed the duality of sale and purchase, supply and demand for millennia. The Nehushtan itself, if taken as a representation of serpent versus serpent, is an image of renewal reminiscent of the caduceus. For all the

---

[43] P. Hemenway, The Secret Code: The mysterious formula that rules art, nature, and science (London, 2008).
[44] Ibid. p.3.

evils of money in the degradation of humanity, reciprocity has been the balancing principle between 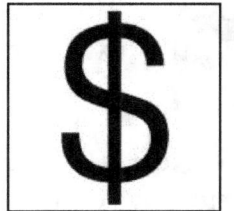 greed and need, and it is in this sense that the serpent-pole is recognised as a symbol of plenitude and self-generating renewal. Today 86% of all foreign exchange trade is in American dollars and the United States is the richest and most powerful empire in history. Few people would realise that the dollar sign is an image of the serpent-pole, but that is precisely what it is.

It will be recalled that in ancient times the caduceus was carried by a *kēryx*, the trusted messenger retained by the city state. Over time, a class of *Kērykes* developed, with sacred and highly secret duties connected with the Eleusinian Mysteries. They were known as the sons of Hermes, and guided initiates along the only paved road in ancient Greece, the *Kukeion* ("Sacred Way") which led from Athens to the city of Eleusis, site of the Rites of Demeter. The *Kērykes* popularized the cult and allowed many more to be initiated into the great secrets of Demeter and Persephone, the gods associated with fecundity, life, and death.

It is said that the dollar sign evolved from the "*P*" used to represent Spanish pieces of eight coins in the Americas, known as Spanish dollars, and that the earliest US coins did not carry symbols at all until the 1790s. If we accept this as unsatisfactory explanation, determining why the serpent-wand appeared at all as the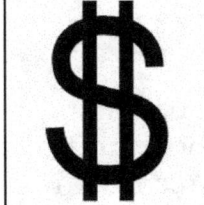

symbol for American currency is the mystery. Indeed, the symbol goes beyond simply being the healing caduceus, as the dollar is often shown with two corresponding columns running through the twisting serpent "S".

The significance of this cannot be lost on us. By the late eighteenth century, the post-revolutionary United States emerged as a prosperous nation state and regional power. Its founding fathers to a man were Christians familiar with the Bible, and many were also freemasons. In freemasonry, the two pillars represent universal duality, often conveyed by the contrasting colours of black and white. They were also men of learning and understood the significance of the caduceus to the *Kērykes*, the messengers of the gods. We see in the dollar sign two opposing forces of division, and without which there can be no equilibrium and balance.

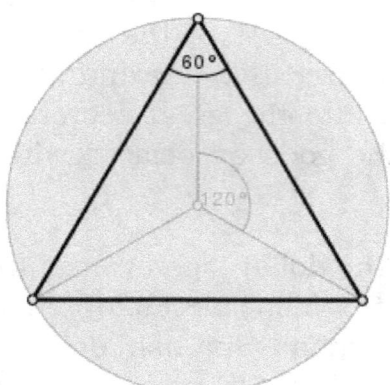

For instance, the beginning of American global hegemony came about in the 1944 Bretton Woods Accord. The ostensible goal of the Accord was to prevent the undermining of international currencies, but this came at the expense of British dominance, which at that time covered a fifth of the globe and one quarter of its population. The principle feature of Bretton Woods was the adoption of a monetary policy maintaining an international exchange rate tied to the US dollar. The Accord also created the International Monetary Fund (IMF) and the World Bank both of which are still with us today and which underpin the economic power and authority of the United States.

In Kabbalistic terms, the twin columns or pillars of Solomon's Temple are represented by the Hebrew letter *daleth*, the letter for strength and immutability. The third component, the serpent or "S" interposed on these columns represents the equilibrium of the dual forces over which America holds global dominance. The metallic serpent on the Nehushtan was cast from copper or bronze, so that those who were stricken by the fiery snakes could look upon something of value, then we can see how the same holistic power is bestowed on the holder of the dollar, figuratively the third pillar (the number 3) of a materialistic, worldly trinity. The question as to whether there is an operative or magical power in the confluence of the dollar symbol can be debated, but that discussion lies outside the scope of this book and the  knowledge of the author. However, the number 3 in a numerological context symbolises manifestation, and it is often represented by the geometric equilateral triangle, which has three sides of the same length.

Taking the Hermetic principle "as above, so below" and the fact this expression denotes the dual nature of the two columns in equilibrium, we end up with the Seal of Solomon. It seems odd that the numbers 2, 3 should equate to a six-sided symbol when reflected in and upon itself, but applying the principles outlined above, that is exactly what happens.

Shortly after Bretton Woods, U.S. President Harry S. Truman established a special cabinet committee to discuss the future of Palestine, which in May 1946 announced its approval to admit 100,000 refugees into the Mandate. Within five years of the Bretton Woods Accord, the state of Israel was established on 29 November 1947 (2+9+1+1+1+9+4+7=33; and 3+3=6), when the United Nations adopted Resolution 181 to divide Palestine.

On 14 May 1948 (1+4+0+5+1+9+4+8=32; and 3+2=5) Israel declared itself an independent state, and the United States recognized it on the same day. It may be a flight of fancy, but not only is thirty-two the mirror of twenty-three, but the numerological numbers for the UN Resolution (6) and Israeli independence (5) become the number eleven, the twin columns or pillars of duality representing the celestial ether from which the elements are said to have been produced. The alchemical symbols for the elements are a series of triangles, that pointing upwards represents the direction of the volatile elements in the force of nature (air and fire), and that pointing downward the fixed passive elements (water and earth). The line across air and water signifies the mystical union of both the volatile and fixed forces in nature; the predominance of the large segment in the middle the control of elemental nature imbued with the fifth element of the spirit. The conquest of the Promised Land is said to figuratively represent the future reintegration of the essences of matter into its principle, the *prima materia,* at the end of time.

4 | The Tree of Life

Jacques de Livron Joachim de la Tour de la Casa Martinez de Pasqually (Martinez de Pasqually, 1708-1774) was the son of Don Martinez Pasqualis, originally of Alicante, in Valencia, and was of Sephardic Jewish ancestry. Pasqually was a nobleman and a cavalry officer, and in 1768 met the "unknown Philosopher", 25-year-old Louis-Claude de Saint-Martin, a young army officer and fellow freemason. Pasqually taught Saint-Martin that humanity retained vestiges of Adam's original supernatural powers, often referring to the direct communications he received from angels and spirits. Pasqually's tract entitled *The Treatise on the Reintegration of Beings into their Original Estate, Virtues and Powers, Both Spiritual and Divine* was an exegesis of the book of Genesis, albeit not completed by his death.

In his Treatise Pasqually sets out a cosmogony wherein, before time existed, God "emanated" from within himself spiritual beings intended to form a loving family about him. These emanated beings were of different classes or grades, and certain of them "prevaricated" (rebelled) against him, having conceived in their thoughts the belief they were God's equals. This is what Pasqually termed "the principle of spiritual evil." In response, God created a physical universe of time and matter to be a prison to contain their malice. Saint-Martin therefore learned from Pasqually that the creative void or primeval "chaos" from which the emanated beings and the universe came into existence was the *prima materia*, the very substance of the Divinity. The *prima materia* was the unity of consciousness, and to know himself, the Creator separated and created the celestial beings to operate a "cult" of worship about him. The universal prison God then created to contain the beings that turned away from him to their pride, was produced by the energy or movement of the Divine consciousness (Mind) and the *prima materia* to generate the elements of fire, air, water, and earth. The fifth element was the ether or unchanging *prima materia* itself, a vital force breathing life into the universe:

> "For I the Lord do not change; therefore you,
> O children of Jacob, are not consumed."
> Malachi 3:6

The "fiery serpents" in the wilderness are an allegory for the harmful, fallen seraphs or spirits described by Pasqually. In the friction between order and chaos, good and evil etc in the myth played out in the plague at Edom, we discover that to enact true change on the physical plane, it is necessary to be in communion with the mental and spiritual planes too. This was achieved in Pasqually's system through detailed and highly secretive theurgical workings which mirrored the priestly operations of the Levites.

Pasqually taught that Moses was an allegory of Adam, and the Hebrews were archetypes of the superior beings sent to command the rebellious angels.[45] According to Pasqually, God "emanated" man with the same virtues and powers that the fallen angels enjoyed, so as to reconcile them to God. Originally clothed in an immutable and glorious form, Adam held authority over the created universe for the express purpose of restoring these fallen angels to the love of God. What, then, is it that makes man in the image of God? It is the mind. The mind of man as the image of God (or *imago dei*) was considered by St. Augustine (354-430). He identified three cognitive acts: awareness of an object, internal image or concept; a cognitive faculty formed by the object; and free will to make the cognitive faculty turn to its object. St. Augustine contended that only memory, self-knowledge and love were those aspects which made humanity in the image of God The "triadic mind" was therefore reflected in the imagery of a father, mother, and child (equating to mind, knowledge, and love, as well as memory, intellect and will).

The transmutation of the mind is thereby effected through the dissolution of fixed thinking, into a different mental vibration and shifting our way of perceiving things. Thus, Moses' Raised Serpent symbolised his authority over the fiery seraphs so that to look upon it was sufficient to be psychologically protected from their malignance and harmful insinuations. Pasqually wrote:

> "The mischievous spirit insinuated to Adam its demoniac power. Adam...resolved to operate the demoniac science rather than

---

[45] Pasqually, M, de *Treatise on the reintegration of Beings into their Priginal Estate, Virtues and powers, Both Spiritual and Divine* 1775 (Anon. Translation).

the divine science which the Creator gave him...He rejected entirely his own spiritual divine thought in order to use that which the mischievous spirit had suggested to him."

The Raised Serpent is talismanic and binds evil spirits, preventing them from causing harm, thereby balancing the sufferings of the people, like the grumbling of the people over the lack of food and water, was a direct consequence of the negative energies of the demonic spirits, who "bit" their victims in the same way that Adam ate from the Tree of Knowledge of Good and Evil. This resulted in the previously unblemished and incorruptible state of man becoming trapped in its present material form, subject to the universal laws of time, decay, and death.

The Treatise expounds on Pasqually's concern to reconcile the world – mired as it is in decay and chaos as a result of the fall of man - with God. For this, he turns to the legend of the "perfect reconciliation" of Abel (the "child of peace"). Adam tried to persuade his firstborn, Cain, to emulate the works and spiritual functions of his younger brother, Abel, who had acquired the means of direct communication with the Divine via magic and superior knowledge. This was why God favoured him, and it was not out of favouritism. It was simply that Cain surrounded himself with an impenetrable barrier of ignorance. Cain persevered in the principle of spiritual evil and offered Abel as a sacrifice to the prince of demons.

Following Abel's murder by Cain, Adam was at his lowest state of rejection and hardship. This was because the harmonised trinity or perfect geometric triangle required to point upwards to God had been destroyed and was imbalanced.

The Temptation by Hans Holbein the Younger

Remember, we need to allegorise the characters of Adam, Cain and Abel as Cause, Effect and Outcome. However, Seth (Adam's third son) enjoyed some (but not all) of Abel's inherent psychic powers, and while he was not fully reconciled until the advent of the Son of Man in the form of Christ, the process of reintegration with the Creator was finally under way. The descendants of Cain lacked these spiritual gifts. It became necessary for God to manifest himself in material creation to repair the link between both branches of man in his fallen state and that of his original image. Therefore, the Raised Serpent's image may have reminded the people of Seth, from whom they were descended, since he replaced Abel and restored hope. In the same way, despite the incarnation of Christ, Pasqually taught that the "prevarication of man" would persist until all the sons of Adam had been reconciled:

> "...the Christ has reconciliated with God the Father only those who have been marked by the seal of the spiritual operation of the righteous. This seal was visibly sent to them without mystery about the way they would have to use it on behalf of those who ought to receive it so that they can be more fortified in the faith and the mercifulness of the Creator, and also to be able to sustain with invincible strength the powerful manifestation of the divine justice which ought to be operated in front of them by the Christ among all the inhabitants of the earth living in divine privation." [46] Martinez de Pasqually

The operations of the ascended Christ were therefore twofold: firstly, to reconcile humanity by a restoration of the link with Adam, and secondly by empowering the "saint patriarchs" of an elect priesthood descended from Seth and marked out by God for the purpose. The essence of this restoration (for the individual as well for the whole of humanity), was to return to man some of

---
[46] Ibid pp. 20-24.

his original psychic gifts, thereby reintegrating each individual human soul. If we consider that simply "to look" upon the image of the Brazen Serpent could heal, then we must acknowledge there was a psychic process at play. This psychic healing did not seek to replicate primal man but to adapt humanity to its present condition in the wilderness i.e., the material universe. The Nehushtan activated some of the same "Divine forces" that Adam once enjoyed. These energies were required for man's first work, but they also helped to defend the people from the fiery serpents afflicting them.

And Elohim Created Adam by William Blake

In terms of the numerological considerations discussed previously, the pride and fall of man equates to the opposing processes of cause, effect, and suffering. Pasqually passed on an occult doctrine of numbers to his initiates, and which influenced the writings of Saint-Martin, of which A.E. Waite would write:

> "We have every reason to suppose that it was confined to attaching certain mystical ideas to certain numbers, and in this respect it is certainly of very high interest to the occult student, because its numerical mysticism is quite opposed to that of other known school, especially in its treatment of the quinary as an evil number."[47]

That said, for Pasqually's student, Louis-Claude de Saint-Martin (1743-1803), numbers were symbols or

metaphors for the essential character or energy of the form they represent. Born at Amboise, France, into the minor nobility, Saint-Martin came to develop a distinct cosmology from his master. For him numbers were neither inherently good nor evil. The number two was nevertheless regarded by him as a negative power "serving the receptacle of all the scourges of diving justice"[48], and three in

---

[47] Op. Cit. Waite, The Life of Louise Clade de Saint-Martin etc. p.393.
[48] Ibid.

Saint-Martin's system "operate[d] the direction of forms in the celestial and terrestrial"[49] and was therefore the number by which the elements of bodies are composed. The combined number of our present condition, the consequence of sin, or five, was the exception, however, and regarded by him as an "evil number". However, that is only half the story, because there is a corresponding restoration or ascension from this condition through the grace of God. As we shall see in the following chapter, this number is also used by the good spiritual beings assuming the form and character of the material encampment, so as to enable them to descend into the "infected region" of evil occupied by humanity. This, you may recall, is essentially what the Tower card in the Tarot deck represents. The Nehushtan, the *serpens mercurii*, was achieving just this, firstly by its resemblance to the true angelic form of the seraphim imposing the authority of God over the fallen entities, and also through the intuitive knowledge held by the people "looking" upon it. This was a form of appropriating to the fallen state of man a personal reconciliation.

Saint-Martin emphasised this cosmology in his treatise *Man: His True Nature & Ministry:*

> "For if, strictly speaking, two things may be respectively the other to each other, there is, nevertheless, a priority between them, either in fact, or conventionally, which requires the second to be considered as the other in respect to the first, and not the first as the other in respect to the second; for, that

---
[49] Ibid.

which is first is one, and can offer no difference, having no point of comparison anterior to itself, whereas that which is second finds that point of comparison before it. Such is the case with the two worlds in question; and I leave it to the reader to compare the light and certainties we find in the metaphysical order, or what we call the other world, with the obscurities, approximations, and uncertainties we find in the one we inhabit; and I also leave it to him to pronounce whether the world we are not in has not some right to priority over that we are in, as well on account of the perfections and science it affords us, as of the superior antiquity it seems to have over this world of a day in which we are imprisoned."[50]

Man can only hope for direct communication with Divinity after his reconciliation, and which cannot be made perfect during our present material course. For the Martinists, therefore, the Divine Code is a means by which man can use certain methods and innate abilities to invoke Divine and angelic assistance. Hezekiah's reforms, if such they were, appeared to be an attack on such intermediary forms, which he regarded as superstition and the weakening of humanity's resolve to follow the immutable Law of God. In contrast, the mastery of true religion was held to comprise the following principles: (1) understanding or gnosis of the material universe; (2) knowledge of the existence of the good and evil spirits, and the original unfallen state of man; (3) knowledge of God. For all the

---

[50] Ibid. pp.19-20

importance of the Nehushtan in the Temple courtyard it was, ultimately, a mere thing of brass in the mind of Hezekiah and no substitute for the Law. It therefore had to go, along with any other objects that attracted "misguided" veneration. The fact that these objects might be melted down to help pay-off the Assyrians was a bonus factor, but not necessarily the only one.

The Creation

The realms of both nature and spirit are subject to their own immutable laws. In Emanuel Swedenborg's cosmology, creation has a divinely established order that starts with God and descends through the heavens and the world of spirits, until it reaches the natural world, which is the level at which things have physical existence. Each of these levels is a less perfect reflection of the one above it. The very existence of patterns in nature is suggestive of this order and structure, the obvious outcome of generative creative processes. Cain and Abel are allegories of the opposing cosmological forces of materialism and spirit. We have seen how in the gnostic tradition of early Christianity, and as taught by Martinism today, the rebellious spirits (the fiery seraphs) were cast from heaven and incarcerated within the confines of time and elemental matter, the created universe. Here they were free to act out their malice without consequence, but it was nonetheless a prison. In case you have not already noticed, I should point out that the main theme of this book concerns the doctrine of choice. The main difference between the exoteric Christian view of free-will and that in Martinism is that in the latter mankind is not entirely at liberty to exercise it. This is because of the influence these fallen angelic beings exert on the intellect (mind) of man. Hence the phenomena of demonic possession and a whole raft of mental illnesses. If we can accept that fallen spirits influence the thoughts and consciousness of human beings, then we can also accept that they can corrupt us.

Pasqually described how the fallen seraphs as the "creators" of evil thought continually strive to insinuate their evil intellect around the corporeal form of man. For Pasqually, the soul, thus influenced, drives away the good spiritual beings, and unites instead with that which it has freely preferred. To withstand being possessed by the fallen entities of the first emanation, or at least being influenced by them, it is necessary to call upon and be assisted by the higher beings still in communion with God. This was the sole reason and purpose of operative magic in Pasqually's system, which preserved much of the Levitical magic of the long-lost Jerusalem Temple, preserved in rabbinical Judaism.

The raised serpent in the Biblical book of Numbers is essentially a talismanic energy which acts to screen the negative impressions emanating from the demons frustrating the will of God. We may recall that according to the Pythagoreans five represented the marriage or harmony of the dual aspects of nature and spirit, that is of the four elements in nature plus the addition of spirit, the fire-like substance of the supernatural.

The Tree of Life: 19th century Bible illustration

In the Nehushtan, therefore, we see the following five elemental configurations:

- the pole representing earth;
- the bronze serpent representing the unification of water and fire ("except a man be born of water and of spirit he cannot enter into the kingdom of heaven." John 3:5);
- the raising of this fiery water in a movement upwards, the "wind" (*"the wind bloweth where it listeth, and thou hearest the sound thereof, but canst not tell whence it cometh, and whither it goeth: so is every one that is born of the Spirit."* John 3:8); and

- the spiritual and supernal "marriage" of mind with spirit; that is, of man with God.

We see five elemental component parts, the four natural elements, and spirit in conjunction. These dual aspects of the number five (4+1) represent the positive upward pointing or "raised" pentagram in geometrical terms, and which force or power (Greek: *dunamis*) influences the people beholding it. It acts to supress, weaken, and dismiss the negative seraphs tormenting the people. In a sense, it is a psychological screen and the positive aspect of two and three (or twenty-three) as the manifestation of Divine cause and effect in the world, with the promise of man's restoration to his original place at the centre.

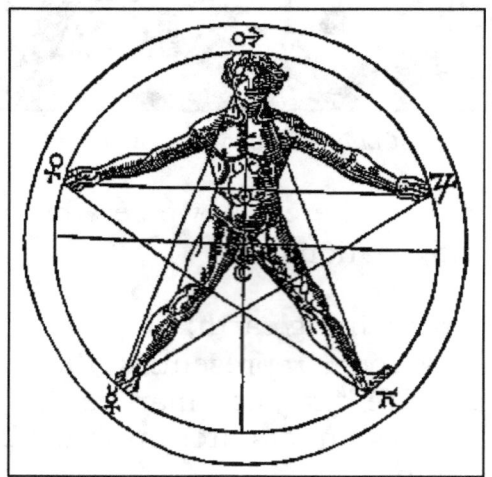

However, as we have seen, the numerical system employed by Louis-Claude de Saint-Martin suggests that he did not regard number five as the sign of the microcosm of man, but instead as an especially evil number:

"It is said that 2 becomes 3 by its minus, 3 becomes 4 by its centre, 4 is falsified by its double centre, which makes 5, and 5 is imprisoned by the measure 6,7,8,9,10, which forms the corrective and rectifier of the evil quinary. The number also connects with what Saint-Martin has to tell us concerning the two-fold application of all numerals. True numbers produce invariably life, order and harmony; thus they always act for, and never against, even when they serve as the scourges of justice ... False numbers, on the contrary, produce nothing; they may ape but cannot imitate the true; they manifest in dismemberment, never in generation, because they have become false by division and have lost the capacity for engendering."[51]

The above description certainly fits with many of the discordant experiences associated with the numbers five or twenty-three as outlined in the first chapter, and also that of the Hebrews in the wilderness afflicted by the curse of fiery serpents. However, as with so much else in the arena of the Divine Code, there is a caveat: that which A.E. Waite described as the difference between false numbers "being employed to operate restoration" and "those operating their own injustices."[52] As he explained:

---

[51] Ibid. pp. 405-406.
[52] Ibid. p.406.

"In the latter case they are given over to themselves and separated wholly from their true line; in the former case, true being assumes their form and character so as to descend into their infected region."[53]

Mashiach

This double application of number in the Divine Code may explain how the Nehushtan was perceived as a precursor of the *Mashiach* (Messiah). If the icon was identified with the promise of a Divinely "anointed" or "chosen" future king and deliverer of Israel, then this is most likely why it was venerated in the temple courtyard. It also gives us the strongest clue yet as to why it was torn down by Hezekiah, since it represented the hope of an alternative form of kingship to his own. The Messianic Age of the Christian era perceives the Messiah universally, not as a human king of Israel but as the Second Adam, a being of both seemingly incompatible Divine and human natures. This Divine Man has not removed the source of suffering; but has enabled his followers to survive it by trusting in God and the hope of reconciliation with him.

It is this context that the Messiah equates with the Nehushtan. The episode of the plague of fiery serpents is allegorical of the fallen condition of humanity. The people were tormented and subjected to the malignant forces of chaos of the fallen seraphim, who operated their will upon the minds of men. In so doing they created a barrier or envelope, separating human

---
[53] Ibid.

consciousness from the immensity of the Divinity. The plague represented the darkest state of humanity trapped in elemental nature, represented by the influence of the power of the number five, being the number of fallen man's physical form and the chief source of his suffering. It is this which makes mankind susceptible to the psychic influences of the fallen spirits, who act as humanity's tormentors. The psychic envelope around people intercepts and interrupts the communication of God's light and wisdom. Only thoughts which are good and just can be projected into physical matter to break and dissipate that barrier. The Nehushtan enabled that as a precursor of the grace of restitution found in the cross.

Jung was interested in a causal connection between mind, spirit and matter, and referred to it as a "projection" of the unconscious identity between the psyche and the spirit imprisoned in matter.[54] The restoration of the intimate connection and likeness of the mind of man with God is the key transformative process sought in alchemy. "Looking upon" the innate spirit in matter with the right intention is a projection or action of the Great Work. In this context, the Nehushtan could best be described as a "container" for the processes of the thought and intellect of those acting upon it, both human and Divine, such that the healing experienced by the Hebrews was, in truth, not a cure for lethal snake bites but a symbol of reintegration with God. Jung would write:

---

[54] C. G. Jung, *Psychology and Alchemy* (Second Ed., London 1968), p.267.

> "The assumption underlying this train of thought is the causative effect of analogy. In other words, just as in the psyche the multiplicity of sense perceptions produces the unity and simplicity of an idea, so the primal water finally produces fire, i.e., the ethereal substance – not (and this is the decisive point) as a mere analogy but as a result of the mind's working on matter."[55]

We are left with a situation where Divinity had to assume the form and character of a human being to descend into "the infected region" of physical matter to cure it. This was not unlike the process of inoculation involving antivenom. In the narrative of the burning bush, we noted the encampment of Divinity in nature, and in the residence of the Shekinah in the Ark of the Covenant.

However, with the Nehushtan the evil forces of the false number five are brought under control by the manifestation of Divine Power in imitation of their own form. The Nehushtan embodied both the metallurgical work of the artificers and the projection of the people's will upon it. It therefore encapsulated a transformation of physical matter through chemical processes as well as by the individual and collective psyche of the people. In this sense it was nothing short of a symbol of the coming Messiah into our place of exile (infected region).

Where this leads us is not a matter of conjecture. If we regard humanity as a spiritual, disembodied being "encamped" in sensory matter, trapped in the flesh,

---

[55] Ibid. p. 269.

then it is not such a wild flight of fancy to regard the universe as the source of suffering.

The "twenty-three enigma" is essentially a code reminding us of our true nature as a spiritual being, subject to the material laws of nature, deprived of our identity and given over to demonic forces. However, this is a dispensation over which the Creator still retains supreme control.

Imagine, if you will, how the Nehushtan appeared after it was torn down by Hezekiah. The wooden pole and bronze serpent broken apart and in pieces. If you were to resurrect the Nehushtan in the privacy and space of our mind, you might equate the pole with your physical body, that which can be penetrated by good or bad influences. The restoration is not something you can do on your own, in exactly the same way that the form of the body cannot come into existence alone, without genetic parents. This is the real meaning of Pasqually's doctrine of choice, wherewith we become free of the insinuations of evil by calling upon the assistance of higher beings to liberate our thoughts and participate in our liberation.

With help we may reattach the copper serpent to the pole, and the two once again become conjoined and inseparable. Imagine this reunited image as a single unity, a marriage of your thought and will. When you raise this imagined image of the restored Nehushtan, you may feel how this action of *movement* becomes a third force.

This self-initiatory exercise should open in you a greater awareness of the numinous.

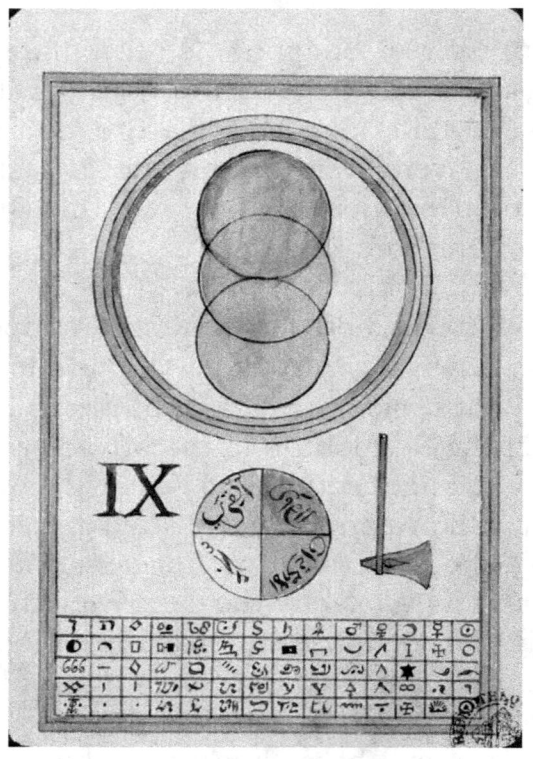

Photo : Médiathèque Jacques-Chirac, Troyes Champagne Métropole

You will recall that for the Pythagoreans the number two was the number of movement symbolizing duality, and when these two opposites were merged, their energy generated the attributes of the number three. We can liken the pole and serpent to two geometric circumferences conjoined, at whose centre is formed the Vesica Piscis, representing the Kingdom of God. The faithful looking up to God are a third, overlapping circumference. This image can be found in esoteric art. For example, the image opposite contains ciphers appearing in the mysterious eighteenth-century manuscript, *La Tres Sainte Trinosophe*.

This image is highly esoteric, and represents the material universe and the interaction of the spiritual realms about it. It describes the form or "envelope" (barrier) around mankind (represented by the number nine, that of excess and dissolution), which acts to intercept the communication of God's light. For that junction to occur, only the right action of man can break and dissipate this barrier. It is only by an act of free will, unsullied by demonic influences, that he can be regenerated. It is for humanity to take up the axe illustrated above, and become the destroyer of that envelope of corruption surrounding the Four Worlds of emanation, creation, formation and manifestation (the material universe) designated by the circle of four quarters in the image.[56] It is essentially a cipher presenting us with a code as to how to free the divinity trapped within our material confines.

This is a process of thought restoring the Nehushtan in the mind, and mirrors the Thought, Will and Action of the Divine consciousness itself:

> "In the beginning was the Word, and the Word was with God, and the Word was God. The same was in the beginning with God. All things were made by him; and without him was not anything made that was made. In him was life; and the life was the light of men. And the light shineth in darkness; and

---

[56] A.E. Waite, The Holy Kabballah: A Study of the Secret Tradition in Israel (London, 1924) p.197

the darkness comprehended it not." John 1:1-5

There, in the wilderness, half a millennia before Christ, a prototype Messiah was raised in the form of the Brazen Serpent carried before the people, as a manifestation of the Divine Presence and precursor of the material incarnation. There is no other meaningful explanation, because the flame of the burning bush represented the *prima materia* and Presence of God himself in the material plane, amidst which stood the bush as a metaphor of the Tree of Life. The Nehushtan figuratively represented the Divine flame both in its shiny brassiness and colour, and also by way of its creation in the foundry fire. The pole to which it was affixed similarly represented the Tree of Life. Carried aloft, it also signified the summit of Mount Horeb, where the covenant was delivered to the people. The burning bronze will have cast light all about it, into the darkness at night, and by reflection of the Sun by day.

> "Nebuchadnezzar the king was astonished, and rose up in haste, and spake, and said unto his counsellors, Did not we cast three men bound into the midst of the fire? They answered and said unto the king, True, O king. "Look!" he answered, "I see four men loose, walking in the midst of the fire; and they are not hurt, and the form of the fourth is like the Son of God." Daniel 3:24-25

The metal assaying was a petition to God and an attempt to encounter the Divinity. The furnace into which Daniel was thrown, the burning bush of Moses and the ovens of the ancient alchemists, were essentially the same thing: portals through which the Divine fiery substance communicated with man. In that sense the layer between the material world and the spiritual realm became very "thin". Thus, if we think of the fiery serpents and the Brazen Serpent as a symbol of triumph over the opposing forces of order and chaos, good and evil, light, and dark, life and death etc, the Tree amidst it is the path or ladder

Daniel's Furnace by Hans Holbein the Younger

of return leading to the Divinity. This duality between life and death or slavery and freedom is not unlike a mirror or burnished bronze shield, reflecting pure light. These opposing forces are represented in a state of timeless harmony and balance, represented by the combined image of the Nehushtan, which signifies the mystical marriage of opposites and the power of serpent over serpent. The reconciliation of these dual forces is mirrored in the pole, where the serpent entwines itself in a glorious and incorruptible body of burnished metal. In the same way the incarnation of the Son of Man is the union of two incompatible halves, that of Spirit with the material "seed of woman", the human mind and body.

The Most Holy Trinosophia, one of the most enigmatic and challenging of the occult masterpieces of the eighteenth-century revival in France, the image of the burnished bronze serpent stands out. The description of this in the text is that of an altar in the shape of a snake, made of greenish gold and a description referring to it as "the serpent of desire." The sword, like the axe above, is to be drawn to strike the serpent and to be liberated from the evil entities beset it.[57]

The Beast of Revelation

In the Book of Revelation, John of Patmos describes a serpent or "dragon" with seven heads and ten horns which he identifies with Satan (Revelation 12:9). This image of the serpent symbolizes the political dominions enslaving and repressing man's original freedoms and power. On each of the seven heads of the serpent are diadems or crowns, representing the seven kingdoms (that is, Egypt, Assyria, Babylon, Persia, Greece, Rome - and an empire yet to come). Five of these kingdoms had already fallen at the time of John, and the Roman Empire has since fallen. The ten horns on the dragon represent rulers of the future, seventh kingdom, and who will come to power in the epoch of the Antichrist. Therefore, immanent within the Serpent is an eleventh ruler of the seventh and final kingdom. It follows that

---

[57] See my *The Most Holy Trinosophia – A Book of the Dead* (New York, 2021) pp.191-195.

there are really eleven horns, albeit only ten are visible. You may recall the significance of the number fifty-six in Martinism, which is a geometrical label for conflict, duality and Armageddon. The number eleven represents order and chaos in conflict, from which war and terrible suffering results. The number of death. However, in contrast, the ten sephiroth of the Tree of Life contain a concealed sephira, known as Da'at. Da'at is a portal, the location of a mystical state in the Tree of Life, wherein all ten sefirot are in unity and harmonised. Essentially the Divine Unity (10=1+0=1) is engendered by the circular self-generating principle, or sex energy, and Da'at is in truth not a sephirot but the double energy of indivisibility and perfect balance. The positive connotation of the numbers one and ten represent unity. The opposite forces of the Anti-Christ are is therefore order, strength and altruism.

How can this apparent contradiction in the Tree of Life be? The answer is simple, since it is the opposing branch of the Tree of Knowledge of Good and Evil, which has a corresponding negative side, mirroring the Etz Hayim. This is demonstrated numerically by 10 + 1 = 11, and 1+1=2, wherein eleven and two are the numbers of opposition, or chaos and order. We are also reminded of the numerical system of the Marquis de Sade, since the seven kingdoms and eleven kings equate to the number nine, lucid control of which he believed would guarantee a transition to 'improved' conditions in the next life, thus 7 +11=18, and 1+8=9. Indeed, the "Number of the Beast" in Revelation equates to nine, since 6+6+6=18, and 1+8=9).

*Photo Médiathèque Jacques-Chirac,
Troyes Champagne Métropole*

There is, however, the middle way or path mediating between the pathways of opposition, and which we can but dimly perceive from below. This mediating or connecting aspect takes numerical form in the third Hebrew letter, *gimel*, connecting these opposing realms. The number three generated from such interaction completes the two columns and figuratively may be said to unite them into a geometric triangle. The downward pointing triangle of the Divinity acts as a bridge with man once the upward movement of our thought, will and action is completed by "looking up" in faith, which operation connects and completes the two. The number three therefore has a unifying element, just like the sephira Da'at. We can now begin to more fully understand the value attributed to the number three arising out of two.

Order in Chaos

> "And there shall come forth a rod out of the stem of Jesse, and a Branch shall grow out of his roots." Isaiah 11:1

Up to this point, I have avoided providing anything more than a cursory reference to the Kaballah and Gematria (the method of interpreting scriptures through numerical value to Hebrew letters and words). Reserving this discussion for the concluding part of this book was intentional, because the preceding themes required to be as unsullied as possible by Jewish and early Christian mysticism. These must, however, have the final word (as well they should) given the journey thus described. Let us begin with the following passage from the Gospel of Matthew:

> "So all the generations from Abraham to David are fourteen generations; and from David until the carrying away into Babylon are fourteen generations; and from the carrying away into Babylon unto Christ are fourteen generations." Matthew 1:17

Biblical scholars have challenged the historicity of this genealogy ever since modern Biblical criticism began in the late nineteenth century, but few have considered the occult significance of number in the narrative. Traditionally, the number forty-two was applied to the number of generations from Abraham to Jesus, thus:

14+14+14=42. Forty-two is divided here into three separate branches or distinct blocks of generations. We therefore have the number forty-two comprised of three sets of fourteen. This is the same pattern we see in the genealogy in Matthew 1:17, and clearly there is an attempt to make a Gematria connection of Jesus with the Messiah, by way of reference to the Hebrews' forty years in the wilderness.

You may recall that in Gematria the first ten Hebrew letters are given the values of one through ten; the next eight letters are given number values that increase by a factor of ten from twenty to ninety, and the final four letters are given number values that increase by a factor of one hundred to four hundred. Christian theologians were aware of the significance of number in the Gospels, yet failed to tackle them because of the overriding message of justification by faith alone, and the rejection of the Mosaic Law. Why bother with ciphers and codes when the cross alone is sufficient? The important point, however, is that the earliest Christians were predominantly Jews, and it was only within the confines of Judaism that Messianic doctrine was understood or could be interpreted. This also explains the rapid spread of Christianity throughout the Jewish diaspora of the ancient world. This is a statement of fact, and the soteriological legacy of Judaism - whether one accepts Jesus as the Messiah or not. So, what do these numbers tell us about the Divine Code?. The numerical value of the number forty-two is believed to lie at the root of elemental creation, which explains why the earliest Jewish Christians had no difficulty accepting the incarnation of the Logos. The number forty-two is expressed in Gematria by the letters mem (forty) and bet (two).

In the Pentateuch, the number forty represents spiritual ascent, to "look upwards". In geometry this is in the form of an upward pointing or ascending triangle, representing man's thought, will, and actions. For example, Noah's forty days at sea precede his deliverance; the Hebrews' forty years in the wilderness precedes their entrance into the Promised Land; and Christ's forty days in the wilderness precede the beginning of his earthly ministry. This in turn mirrors the forty days Christ spent teaching his disciples after his resurrection and prior to his ascension.

In Judaism is the mikvah pool is required to contain "forty *seah*" (approximately 580 litres) of water. The uses for the mikvah include the ceremony for menstrual cleansing, and conversion immersion. Immersion in the mikvah is reminiscent of sacramental baptism, and John the Baptist applied immersion to a ceremony of ascent in much the same way. However, it will be recalled that in Graeco-Egyptian Hermeticism the element of mercury is associated with water, and its alchemical symbol is the downward-pointing triangle of God's thought, will and action. Elemental water also represents the body in alchemy, and Jesus' words: "Except a man be born of water and of spirit he cannot enter into the kingdom of heaven" (John 3:5) remind us of this connection. The "downward" movement of God engenders a mystical rebirth with the corresponding upward raising of the body, soul, and spirit of man. Since "spirit" is equated with elemental fire - the fifth element - to be born again is to be engendered of both water and spirit. John's baptism therefore represented the dual aspects of the fiery water manifesting God as he escorted the people out of Egypt (physical matter, i.e. water), to freedom (spirit, i.e. fire). This correspondence explains the hidden significance in the miracles of healing performed by Jesus at the pools used by pilgrims for their ritual purification before entering the Temple enclosure. These include the healing of the paralytic at the Pool of Bethesda ("the House of Mercy") (John 5:2-9), and the rock cut Pools of Siloam ("the Red Pool"), considered by some archaeologists to be the original site of Jerusalem. We should no longer be mystified at the true import of the following words:

> "And as Moses lifted up the serpent in the wilderness, even so must the Son of Man be lifted up: that whosoever believeth in him should not perish but have eternal life." John 3:14-15

The transformation of elemental matter into the fifth element anticipates humanity's return to the original spiritual state enjoyed by Adam before the Tempter-Serpent fall. John's Baptism, like the Nehushtan, prefigures this promise of return through immersion in God's grace.

> "And when he had fasted forty days and forty nights, he was afterward an hungered. And when the Tempter came to him, he said, if thou be the Son of God, command that these stones be made bread. But he answered and said, it is written, Man shall not live by bread

> alone, but by every word that proceedeth out of the mouth of God." Matthew 4:2-4

The narrative of Christ's forty days and nights in the Judean Desert highlights the place of number in the Divine Code. It reminds us that forty is the number of *completion*, in exactly the same way as the terminations of the forty years in the wilderness or the forty days of Noah's Flood. In Gematria, forty represents the man who has been re-born. We also see the contrast of obedience in Jesus' forty days and nights in the wilderness, with the rebellions in the Exodus myth:

> "And the people spake against God, and against Moses, wherefore have ye brought us up out of Egypt to die in the wilderness? for there is no bread, neither is there any water; and our soul loatheth this light bread." Numbers 21:5

When we add the second letter of the Hebrew alphabet, *bet* (the number two) to the letter mem (forty) we have the number forty-two. In the Gematria, bet is the number of man and his original spiritual realm in the fifth element. At the fall of Adam and Eve, the number two came to represent division and opposition to the will of God. Thus, man lost his spiritual body and entered corporal form in the four natural elements, just as the spiritual Garden of Eden was replicated by an elemental form on the site of Mount Moriah in Jerusalem (the Temple Mount) where man was cast.

This dichotomy is highlighted in the contrasting response of Jesus to the "Tempter-Serpent" with that of the Hebrews in the wilderness. His compliance with the will of God casts a poor light on the unfaithfulness of the people in the land of Edom. We can now understand how the personification of the Nehushtan by Jesus is a significant part of the salvation story. The negative "Tempter-Serpent" is still present, as are the fiery serpents who minister unto him, and these may lead to spiritual death, even in the Messianic Age. The remedy, the reconstructed Brazen Serpent in the form of the raised Messiah, remains with us for all time. In Kabbalistic terms, "the Path of the Serpent" on the Tree of Life or Etz Hayim[58] can be represented in both positive and negative ways. There are thirty-two paths. The inverse of thirty-two is twenty-three, and the twenty-third path of the Kaballah is called "the House of Consciousness." On this path the initiate learns that his immortal personality, his soul, or mind, exists between two metaphorical pillars, or columns. These are the intellect and instinct, or man's spiritual and animal natures (otherwise the pillars of fire by night and cloud by day), by which God raised the people's consciousness.

In the Kaballah, these columns are symbolized by the Hebrew letters and the sephira Hod (intellect) and Netzach (instinct). Along the ascending path of reintegration - as opposed to the descending path of encampment in the four alchemical elements - the twenty-third path of the Kaballah takes the initiate to the sephirot Hod to acquire knowledge. This leads to a

---

[58] The Tree of Life or Etz Hayim is a diagram consisting of ten spheres or sephirot symbolizing different archetypes, with twenty-two lines or paths connecting them. The sephirot are often arranged into three columns or pillars.

vision of the "Eternal Splendour" of the opposite pillar of Chessed, or mercy, a harmonisation which leads to Kether, the Kingdom of Heaven (which must first be seen, and from whence the Son of Man descended into lower elemental form).

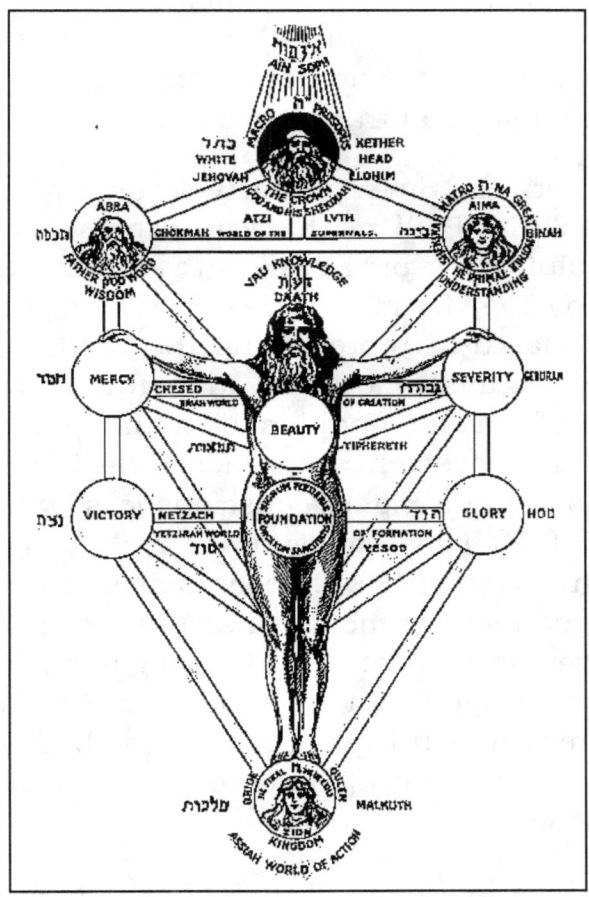

The Tree of Life or Etz Hayim

Hod is the terminus of the Pillar of Severity or Form, the receptacle of the "substance of the Unity", the fifth element of spirit. The opposite pillar of Mercy is the receptacle of the "splendour of the Unity" and the Middle Pillar, the receptacle of "holy power". In Hod, the splendour is only perceived by the intellect, which was Nicodemus' problem. The reflection of this splendour was contained in the burnished bronze of the Brazen Serpent raised by Moses, and then by the Messiah. Thus, it cannot be experienced in its wholeness on earth, and hence why physical death is but the first stage of transformation.

In contrast, the inverse thirty-second path of the Kaballah (the Path of the Tau) represents a much lower evolutionary progression, that from the animal to the spiritual form. The link is that of the lowest sephirot Malkuth, representing the earth, to Yesod, which is located close to Malkuth and permits movement from one condition to another. It is therefore a two-stage movement from elemental form towards the formation of a higher consciousness, which is the promise of what may follow from such progress. The Kabbalistic Tree of Life then branches into the three separate paths or branches of severity, mercy and the middle way or pillar of spiritual enlightenment. There is therefore a significant difference between the inverse twenty-third and thirty-second paths, both of which reflect the interplay of order and chaos within the Divine Code.

In the Gospel of John, Christ's first miracle at Cana immediately precedes the cleansing of the Jerusalem Temple. The proximity between the first miracle and Jesus' most explosive and controversial statements are there for a reason. When Jesus was asked to give a sign proving by what authority he was acting, he clearly wanted those present to hear *the number*. "Destroy this temple, and in three days I will raise it up" (John 2:19). Why three? The first point to note is that there are sixty-six Roman miles between Cana and Jerusalem, something which would not have been lost on the fledgling Johannine community. There are also discrete references to the twelve disciples in the combined narrative. We have previously considered fractal mathematics in numerology, which is a pattern containing smaller and smaller versions of itself. The point of fractal mathematics is the whole pattern. Thus, the genealogy of Jesus was divided into three branches of fourteen, or six (the latter by the formula 1+4+1+4+1+4=15, or 1+5=6) and six is the number of the days of creation. In contemplating what was meant by his reference to the destruction of the Temple and its reassembly in three days, Jesus is alluding to the Fall of Adam and the restoration of the Divine-Man in himself - the Second Adam. If we consider the third branch in the Tree of Life, then we recognise this as the path of grace, and may infer that Jesus intended the reacquisition of man's judgement and union with the Source from which all his thoughts come. To fully appreciate this, let us consider the narrative in John. The combined narrative thinly veils the movement from physical form to spirit by way of the middle pillar in the Tree of Life, and the "three days" are allegories of the three routes man can take for his restoration and that of all nature in the Tree of Life.

> "And the third day there was a marriage in Cana of Galilee; and the mother of Jesus was there. And both Jesus was called, and his disciples, to the marriage. And when they

wanted wine, the mother of Jesus saith unto him, they have no wine, Jesus saith unto her, 'Woman, what have I to do with thee? mine hour is not yet come.' His mother saith unto the servants, 'Whatsoever he saith unto you, do it.' And there were set there six waterpots of stone, after the manner of the purifying of the Jews, containing two or three firkins apiece. Jesus saith unto them, 'Fill the waterpots with water.' And they filled them up to the brim. And he saith unto them, Draw out now, and bear unto the governor of the feast. And they bare it. When the ruler of the feast had tasted the water that was made wine and knew not whence it was: (but the servants which drew the water knew;) the governor of the feast called the bridegroom, and saith unto him, 'every man at the beginning doth set forth good wine; and when men have well drunk, then that which is worse: but thou hast kept the good wine until now.' This beginning of miracles did Jesus in Cana of Galilee and manifested forth his glory; and his disciples believed on him. After this he went down to Capernaum, he, and his mother, and his brethren, and his disciples: and they continued there not many days.

"And the Jews' Passover was at hand, and Jesus went up to Jerusalem. And found in the temple those that sold oxen and sheep and doves, and the changers of money sitting: And when he had made a scourge of small cords, he drove them all out of the temple, and the sheep, and the oxen; and poured out the changers' money, and overthrew the tables; And said unto them that sold doves, 'Take these things hence; make not my Father's house an house of merchandise.' And his disciples remembered that it was written, 'the zeal of thine house hath eaten me up.' Then answered the Jews and said unto him, 'what sign shewest thou unto us, seeing that thou doest these things?' Jesus answered and said unto them, 'Destroy this temple, and in three days I will raise it up'. Then said the Jews, 'Forty and six years was this temple in building, and wilt thou rear it up in three days?' But he spake of the temple of his body." John 2:2-21

If we accept the allegorical interpretation of the three days for man's spiritual passage, as surely we must, then the alchemical marriage of the human soul with the Divine Will is being contemplated. This is the real meaning of the incarnation or double nature of Christ being both human and divine There are six empty stone waterpots, each of which can hold two or three firkins, which is about the forty seah of water used in the Mikvah (hence "after the manner of the purifying of the Jews"). So, the choice of vessel is indicative of the numerical power of creation, generation, and transformation even before the miracle happens. Their number and volume reflect the six days of creation, and movement from one stage of adeptship to another. Jesus asks for the stone waterpots to be filled with water, and by so doing mirrors the creation by giving life to emptiness. The form of water is transformed into an entirely different substance, and one that is of great value at the marriage celebration. Applying fractals, the number six equates to three, and this of course is the sacred Trinitarian number in Christianity. I am not suggesting that John intended to refer to the Trinity, since the development of the formal doctrine took centuries to formalise. Rather I suggest that latent within Johannine cosmology is a tri-fold understanding of the nature of God, and which number repeats itself time and time again, not only in the Bible but within the Divine Code of creation itself. Thus we have Jesus referring to the three days in the tomb before his resurrection; the six days of creation and the twelve tribes of Israel in the same combined narrative.

At the time of the miracle at Cana, ritual cleansing with water was undertaken by the bridegroom on the day of his wedding, a practise still followed in some branches of Judaism today. However, the presiding coen also took a ritual cleansing prior to the recitation of his blessing as well. His blessing was the *nesiat kapayim* ("the raising of hands") and was bestowed from a raised position, reminiscent of the Nehushtan. It recited the blessing on the people by the chief Levite High Priest, Aaron, in the wilderness:

> "The Lord bless thee and keep thee: the Lord make his face shine upon thee, and be gracious unto thee: the Lord lift up his countenance upon thee, and give thee peace." Numbers 6:24-26

The sign that the people ask of Jesus is reminiscent of their attitude in captivity, and most would have missed the significance of the three days of which Jesus' spoke, let alone that by his own power he will be "raised up" for them to look upon. The incredulous crowd remarks that it took forty-six years to build the Temple, a number that will not be lost on the reader of this book, who will recall that there are forty-six chromosomes in each human body made from twenty-three pairs.

Daniel's Vision of the Four Beasts, Hans Holbein the Younger

Perhaps the Temple was always understood to be an allegory of the human form trapped in matter, and just like the stone waterpots at Cana was empty without the Divinity to fill it. Jesus' remarks therefore appear to relate to spiritual and not physical death. The three days relate to the reintegration of man's intellect, thought and will in the resurrection body. Saint-Martin described this path or journey in allegorical terms:

"The presence of the Israelites in the land of Egypt, where they were subjected, may represent man in the bosom of a woman, depriving him of all his faculties, and deprivation, his escape and apprehension, has the aspect of the Egyptians who are the punishers and continuous gaolers of this passing prison. The arch in the middle of the sea is likened to the Spirit, conductor of the mind and our goodly companion, who helps us to make the journey. The passage from the Red Sea can also be envisaged as the passage from this life to the other and is done in the same way, which announces the deprivation we are in. The angel stops in the middle of the sea and supports the waters to favour the passage; it is the Spirit conductor and defender, the good companion. He leads to the port those who follow him with confidence, but he abandons the waters to their natural course for those who disregard or despise him."[59] Louis-Claude de Saint-Martin

A.E. Waite concluded that the Kabballah is conceived or understood in the mind and realised by way of the heart, i.e. feeling.[60] On the duality in *Malkuth*, he wrote of this in terms of the generative or creative opposing forces of the masculine and feminine sex forces we find

---

[59] See my translation in Osborne, M. R. *The Lessons of Lyons* (London, 2021) pp.44-45
[60] Op.Cit. *The Holy Kabballah* pp.289-290

in number and the Divine Code, underpinning the Four Worlds of material creation:

> "... if the temptation and the Fall signify an aberration of sex, a declension or a materialisation therein, there is no question that the Tree of Life is the perfect way of nuptials; and the ascent of the Sephirotic Tree, which – according to the Secret Schools – is a return into union, we shall find at the proper time to be a journey in the graces and glories of the Sacred Shekinah" [61]

This ascent might be likened to a deeper, fully conscious awareness of the Four Worlds of the Kaballah: moral action, the formation of right mindfulness, the creation of the new self and spiritual intimacy with God. This theme is represented by the marriage at Cana and the Presence of God. This perennial movement between the Divine and the material on the middle path is reflected in the allegory of Jacob's Ladder as described in Genesis:

> "And he dreamed, and behold a ladder set up on the earth, and the top of it reached to heaven; and behold the angels of God ascending and descending on it." Genesis 28:12

The movement of looking unto God, is that through which we choose the good, even though we are incapable of fully restoring order over chaos. It is a ladder or raised position by which we may ascend

---
[61] Ibid.. pp.289-290

towards Divine Union. This is nothing more or less than that which the Brazen Serpent represents. It is the promise of a future free of the forces of chaos and in which we fully regain our spiritual memory. The anonymous author of the mediaeval mystical treatise *The Cloud of Unknowing* put it thus:

> "Before ere man sinned, might not will be deceived in his choosing, in his loving, nor in none of his works. For why, it had then by nature to savour each thing as it was; but now it may not do so, unless it be anointed with grace. For oftimes because of infection of the original sin, it savoureth a thing for good that is full of evil, and that hath the likeness of good. And both the will and the thing that is willed, the memory containeth and comprehendeth in it."[62]

---

[62] Anon *The Cloud of Unknowing* Ed. Underhill, E. (London, 1922) p.112.

5 | The Omega Point

"In the beginning God created the heavens and the earth." Genesis 1:1

According to the Mishnah, when the Serpent-Tempter persuaded man to eat from the Tree of Knowledge of Good and Evil in Genesis, it did so by reference to the first seven words of the Bible, thereby mocking the work of the Creator. Each of these words had a magical name and number and, in essence, the Serpent was promising Adam the formula to build his own world.

In English, Genesis 1:1 is made up of ten words, but in Hebrew there are seven. The seven words used at the formation of the universe are structured numerologically on a 4 + 3 = 7 basis, and are symbolised on the candlesticks of the Menorah, one of the ten vessels of the Tabernacle placed in the Holy of Holies in the Jerusalem Temple.[63] It symbolised the seven days of creation and the Light of God. The three Hebrew words corresponding to the first three branches of the original Menorah symbolised what God *did* and *when*; and the three words corresponding to the final three branches tell us what he *created*. The

---

[63] The Menorah, the Table, the Altar, the washbasin and Jug, the Ark and the Curtain, the two cherubs and all in its weight.

fourth word, linking the preceding three acts of God is the seventh branch (in the centre), and has no separate meaning on its own since it is an accusative particle forming the verb "created". The structure of the seven words are:

1	"In the beginning"	feminine noun
2	"created"	verb
3	"God"	masculine noun
4	(not a word)	accusative participle
5	"the heavens"	masculine noun
6	"and"	conjunctive participle
7	"the earth"	feminine noun

A few points immediately stand out. There are six words mirroring the six days' labour, since the Shechinah rests in completeness on the seventh. The six days of creation mirror the six sephiroth above Malkuth, which represents a created universe which could not self-create. Without this, the whole meaning of the sentence would be lost, since the fourth (non) word is the axis or central branch. Finally, there is an equal and well-balanced combination of masculine and feminine powers integrated into the design, reflecting the igniting life-force or sex-energy required for self-generation.

The Zohar describes how this numerical code was placed within creation by God, because each letter of the Hebrew alphabet has a force, channelling life.

Jewish mysticism conveys how the world was created with the "Ten Utterances" or Commandments of God in mind (the *asarah ma'amorot*). Thus, the first words at the beginning of # Genesis are connected to the moral code of the Decalogue[64] brought down from Mount Sinai by Moses.

The Menorah, symbolising here the 22 letters of the Hebrew alphabet

---

[64] The Ten Commandments. Exodus 20:1-17.

If the gematric formula for the seven letters is applied to the first thirty-seven prime numbers (i.e. to the decad, by reason of 3 + 7 = 10), then there are exactly *twenty-three* ways to combine the first verse of Genesis to fit these primes - and each value is used precisely twelve times. In fact, the number thirty-seven is the thirteenth prime number, which numerologically becomes four by reason of 1 + 3 = 4, being the number of the classical elements of which Adam sought control. According to the science of the Chaldeans (10th-to mid-6th BC), the number thirty-seven symbolized the life-force. In Gematria, the number thirty-seven has the numerical value as the name of God in Exodus 3:14, *Ehyeh* ("I Am that I Am").

There exists an interesting relation between the number thirty-seven and 666 and 333 (or 9): from 666 we obtain 6+6+6=18 and 18 x 37 = 666; also 3+3+3=9 and 9 x 37 = 333. This formed a critical part of the Marquis de Sade's obsession with the number nine in numerology. Interestingly, 3 x 7 x 37 = 777, the number many occultists associate with the sum value of the Gematria on the thirty-two paths of the Kabballah. For the Pythagoreans, the union of the feminine and the masculine principles in number was a code for elemental stability. They associated this union with the numbers two and three, with the resultant number five being a fractal of the number one, the perfect number.

The molecular composition of Deoxyribonucleic or DNA is two polynucleotide chains coiling around each other, reminiscent of the myth of the caduceus in the Tiresian legend. On the six branches of the Menorah we observe two opposing parts, namely the attributes and actions of God, and what he created. The third part is the axis or central branch in the centre, unifying the whole. In this context we can see how the two chains in DNA resemble the serpent ouroboros, which consumes and replicates itself in an infinite cycle. In ancient alchemy, the serpent was a sigil symbolising sex energy, and the divine proportion it engendered can be observed in the symmetry immanent in all forms. Is it beyond coincidence that, for the ancient Hebrews and Greeks alike, the fractal reduction of the number twenty-three to the perfect number mirrors the alchemical processes of reintegrating the animating force of life with the *prima materia*?

In geometrical terms, this is stylised as the created *materia* pointing upwards, as if to "look upon" the Divinity. The Divine Principle reaches downwards, thereby producing five points of interaction between nature and spirit, symbolised by the pentagram. The *vesica piscis* represents the balance of these opposing types, being the quaternary outcome in the form of unity, or harmony (the "Kingdom of Heaven" referred to by Jesus). Insofar as the Nehushtan is a geometric type, then it conceals innate within itself the *vesica piscis*.

Numbers therefore help us understand that the personification of evil is an aberration in a universe created by perfect weight, number, and measure. Chaos, on the other hand, is the inevitable consequence of the fall of spirit into matter and is an essential if unpleasant aspect of the regenerative processes required for organic life to exist. Thus, the forces of evil at play in the created universe are manifestations of a virus infecting creation.

Vitalism

> *"Did God really say, 'You must not eat from any tree in the garden?' You will certainly not die. For God knows that when you eat from it your eyes will be opened, and you will be like God, knowing good and evil."*

Vitalism is the theory that organic life is dependent on a force distinct from biology. It lies at the heart of the proposition that spirit is locked in matter. Material science denies the existence of spirit, in much the same way as it rejects the multiverse and the existence of independent vibrational energy. However, the advent of quantum physics in the late twentieth century challenged the once incontrovertible Darwinian view that life and consciousness derive entirely from biological processes. Indeed, quantum mechanics proposes mathematical theories regarding the origins of life that are inconsistent with pure biological materialism. Life, even consciousness, at a quantum level may derive from raw energy in the form of vibrations operating outside the known parameters of time and space. Biologist Robert Lanza (b. 1956) for instance has postulated a form of bio-vitalism based on consciousness operating at a quantum level, with echoes back to the classical vitalism of Newton:

> *"Time is the inner form of animal sense that animates events-the still frames-of the*

spatial world. The mind animates the world like the motor and gears of a projector."

"But perhaps we can grant that something happens when the thinking mind takes a vacation. Absence of verbal thought or daydreaming clearly doesn't mean torpor and vacuity. Rather, it's as if the seat of consciousness escapes from its jumpy, nervous, verbal isolation cell and takes residence in some other section of the theater, where the lights shine more brightly and where things feel more direct, more real. On what street is this theater found? Where are the sensations of life?"[65]

In the first chapter we considered how number represents spirit imprisoned in matter. On a quantum level, while the existence of "dark matter" and "dark energy" is contested in many circles of material science, quantum theorists have concluded that both do exist. Dark matter is most likely comprised of what some quantum physicists call "non-luminous" high-energy particles (i.e., not containing light) that may interact or move randomly through space. Dark energy on the other hand is a type of repulsive force generated by fluctuations on empty space, and for which there is presently no viable explanation. It does however appear to exist and is measurable in terms of the gravitational influences it exerts. What we call spirit, an animate energy existing independently of form,

---
[65] Robert Lanza, Biocentrism: How Life and Consciousness Are the Keys to Understanding the True Nature of the Universe, Dallas, 2009

might well exist too. This would provide explanation for the existence of the paranormal, death survival, miracles and a whole host of other supernatural experiences that science refutes.

Stahl

Vitalism has never been the sole domain of metaphysics or mysticism. Healers and physicians down the centuries have been drawn to similar conclusions, and were often persuaded by them. Georg Ernst Stahl (1660–1734) the German medical theorist, observed that unlike organic bodies which decompose following death, inorganic forms remain stable. One need only compare a dead plant or animal with a rock to appreciate this. Stahl concluded that the decomposition of organic matter derives from its chemical composition and, by deduction, he reasoned that there must be an energy or force latent within organic bodies animating and sustaining them. He identified this force as the *"anima"*, or soul, and which was also a source of self-healing. Stahl's *animia* is reminiscent of Konstantin Korotkov's research of kirlian fields around bodies, which perhaps count among the many spiritual forces humanity can no longer perceive. Stahl essentially identified the *prima materia* or fiery water of alchemy with what he termed the "phlogiston":

> "Briefly, in the act of composition, as an instrument there intervenes and is most potent, fire, flaming, fervid, hot; but in the very substance of the compound there intervenes, as an ingredient, as it is commonly called, as a material principle and as a constituent of the whole compound the material and principle of fire, not fire itself."

Mesmer

Stahl was not alone at the dawn of the age of modern science in holding these views. Franz Anton Mesmer (1734-1815) was born in the year of Stahl's death and took up his academic mantle by reasoning that life was comprised of magnetic forces originating from *outside* the body. It followed that such energy could be harnessed by transference from one form to another, and which Mesmer termed "animal magnetism".

Mesmer became convinced that illness was caused by obstacles in the flow of energy about us, and that unblocking this could be achieved through a conductor, like magnets. The transfer of a force from an inanimate object like the Nehushtan as a source for healing may have caused Mesmer some difficulties to reconcile, since bronze is not a magnetic metal. It is, however, an efficient electrical conductor. However, in Mesmer's day electricity was little understood and commonly referred to as "Newton's Spirit". Sir Isaac Newton (1642-1727) regarded what we now know as electricity to be a fluid responsible for gravity and equated it with the spiritual substance of God. Little did he know that dark energy would account for much of the gravitational influence on matter! Mesmer also interpreted Newton's Spirit as a fluid, fiery water, and his work with magnetism was based on a belief that magnets and the heavenly bodies produced electrical fluids that could interact with the body.

In any event, we need not forget that in alchemy serpent symbolism is represented by mercury. This *serpens mercurii* was understood in Mesmer's time to have beneficial healing properties. Indeed, mercury continues to be used medicinally, notwithstanding its toxicity. For example, it is an ingredient in dental fillings and is an effective antiseptic in small doses. If the Brazen Serpent was indeed a healing force, then what other qualities lay in its composition to reassure the Hebrews of its benevolence? If we look again at the characteristics of bronze, we learn that it is an alloy with less friction than other metals, which expands when solidifying. This makes it ideal for metal working and, by analogy, particularly beneficial for nomadic communities. As for any protective forces, if these could be transferred from one form to another – or at least believed to be – then it is not such a great leap of the imagination to begin to understand how the Hebrews could benefit from it. To ward off the evil eye of Apep at night (when the Spitting Red Cobras of the Sinai would strike), the Nehushtan had the effect of reminding the Israelites of the Divinity within, as in the habitation of God in the burning bush and its mobile counterpart, the Ark of the Covenant.

In alchemy, the combination of the essentials of the *tria prima* becomes the igniting force of the body, just as the angel of the Lord appeared in a flame of fire that consumed nothing about it. By directly and incontrovertibly identifying himself with the serpent raised on the tree, Jesus himself revealed the process of the alchemical transformation of matter into spirit. This is the real meaning of being raised: it is to be healed.

The Noosphere

> "And I saw a new heaven and a new earth: for the first heaven and the first earth were passed away." Revelation 21:1

Pierre Teilhard de Chardin (1881-1955) was a French Jesuit priest, theologian, philosopher, and palaeontologist. At one point, he came close to being caught up in the scandal surrounding the fraudulent 'discoveries' of the amateur archaeologist and palaeontologist Charles Dawson (1864-1916). The most notorious instance of Dawson's fraud was the infamous Piltdown Man hoax, which fooled much of the scientific establishment for some time and forever ruined the reputation of the eminent and highly respected palaeontologist Sir Arthur Woodward (1864-1944).

Teilhard

Teilhard assisted Dawson at the Piltdown excavations and several other digs in southern England, although his complicity with Dawson is unproved.[66]

---

[66] Miles Russell, Piltdown Man: The Secret Life of Charles Dawson, London, 2003.

Nevertheless—and this is the point of mentioning the Piltdown hoax—Teilhard's desire to find the "missing link" in human evolution drove him to make a significant philosophical contribution in later life, when he wrote convincingly about humanity's evolution in terms of a collective development of thought consciousness.

Teilhard's theory of the "Noosphere" has interesting parallels with the concept of the reintegration with spirit that we have discussed. There is also the possibility of deriving from it a "unified theory" of the Nehushtan as a form of collective, self-healing thought-transference. Teilhard identified an evolutionary "sphere of thought" encircling the earth. The Noosphere was held by him to be evolving contemporaneously with the evolution of human consciousness. In a sense, much of what Teilhard foresaw has since manifested in the evolution of the internet and the 'akashic record' of the worldwide web. However, the Noosphere is an aspect of nature arising from the collective human mind. Teilhard argued it was an etheric metaphysical substance enveloping creation, and which was set on a trajectory towards a critical convergence point (assuming humanity is around long enough). Thus, just as there are opposite branches in the Etz Hayim which are in fact one and the same Tree of Life, so does the evolution of the group soul of man simultaneously evolve but acquire ever-greater individuation.

For me, Teilhard's noosphere works as a model if it operates *both* forwards *and backwards.* If we regard humanity as a spiritual being imprisoned in time and space, then our materiality is an *involution* from a point where it was once greatest, and we therefore need to work backwards to the point where the collective consciousness or group-soul of our species was already perfected in the man-god, Adam Kadmon. It is case of restoration, not evolution. However, we are physically and cognitively evolving as an animal species too, and we also operate in time, so our spiritual restoration is matched by a corresponding biological *evolution*, an anomaly that is made possible with the existence of spirit, much like the fiery water of which Christ spoke, and that which the Buddha strove to release when he mistakenly sought to starve his body. If we regard the Noosphere as a process to a point where we *regain* our judgement, then we will no longer be rocked about by chaos and the dicey chances of the universe. Conversely, with the advent of artificial intelligence and the complete mastery of the environment by our species in the future, then an evolutionary mirror point can be attained. Again, provided our species has not destroyed itself in the interim. This, for me, is the essential point. True, this cosmogony contrasts with material science, but modern medical theorists and quantum scientists continue to call the materialist perspective into question too.

In purely anthropomorphic terms, the Nehushtan typifies an evolution of thought development, not only in the therapeutic use of metals at the end of the Bronze and dawn of the Iron Ages, but more particularly in the evolution of collective thinking. Indeed, just like Teilhard's Noosphere, the Nehushtan's journey culminated in its own Omega Point in its destruction by Hezekiah – when Israel were finally ready to depart from idol worship.

The brilliance of Teilhard's doctrine of the Noosphere is that it is knowingly imperfect, and has an in-built tolerance allowing for the evolution of its own parameters. As such, it reconciles the Divine Code with human evolution, and the pattern of number in space and time with nature in a much more meaningful way than we may appreciate. Whether we can fully reconcile the twin pillars of order and chaos or spirit with matter in a unified theory of everything is a moot point. Nonetheless, the Brazen Serpent had a profound meaning as a symbol of God's power and mercy for the Children of Light in the desert. It may not have been their first symbol, for Moses and Aaron had their staves, but it was the first icon and representation in material form of the angelic entities beset them (a prototype of the Ark of the Covenant, the Temple to come and the Messiah). The destruction of the Nehushtan by Hezekiah resonates, because it had become a forbidden symbol in an age where the consciousness of the Israelites had evolved to a point in the Noosphere where they experienced the word of God without recourse to idolatry.

The motif of healing is central, for what is healing if not restoration, and the process of becoming sound and healthy again? It is a recognition that something is broken and needs to be repaired. The Brazen Serpent was a cipher for the Divine Code and concealed within it was the meaning of many of the numbers, codes and geometric patterns found in nature. From that point, at the boundary of the Land of Edom, the act of the victims looking differently at nature would forever restrain the power of the "heavenly executioners." Therein lies the Brazen Serpent's significance as the forerunner of the cross of the Christian faith. In short, the pattern is there to be found, and the raised serpent of Moses reminds us to continue the search for spirit locked in matter. It is a reminder that we must never lose sight of the image of the Mirror of Yahweh, the Architect of Worlds, bestowing life on the formless void.

Uraltes Chymisches Werk by Rabbi Abraham Eleazar, 1735

Selected Bibliography

Anon. *The Cloud of Unknowing* (Ed. Underhill, E., London, 1922

Carter, D. *Marquis de Sade*, London, 2011

Dennis, G. W. *The Encyclopedia of Jewish Myth, Magic and Mysticism*, Second Edition, London, 2016

Josephus, *Jewish Antiquities* (Trans. H.S.J Thackeray, London, 1967

Saint-Martin, L-C. de *Man: His True Nature & Ministry* Trans. Edward Burton Penny, London, 1864

Fanthorpe, L & P. *Mysteries and Secrets of Numerology*, New York, 2013

The 23 Phenomenon | RAWilsonFans.org

Harari, Y. *The Sword of Moses (Ḥarba de-Moshe): A New Translation and Introduction* in *Magic, Ritual, and Witchcraft* (University of Pennsylvania Press, Volume 7, Number 1, Summer 2012) pp. 58-98

Hemenway, P. The Secret Code: The mysterious formula that rules art, nature, and science, London, 2008

Jung, C. G. *Psychology and Alchemy,* Second Ed., London 1968

Jung, C. Synchronicity*: An Acausal Connecting Principle.* (Trans. Hull, R F C, London, 1952

Korotkov, K. *Light After Life* (St. Petersburg, 2014)

Lanza, R., Biocentrism: How Life and Consciousness Are the Keys to Understanding the True Nature of the Universe, Dallas, 2009

Mishnah Rosh HaShanah

Osborne, M. R. *The Lessons of Lyons,* London, 2021

Osborne, M.R. *The Most Holy Trinosophia – A Book of the Dead,* New York 2021

Parnia, S. *The Lazarus Effect,* London, 2013

Pasqually, M, de *Treatise on the reintegration of Beings into their Original Estate, Virtues and Powers, Both Spiritual and Divine* 1775 (Anon. Translation)

Peat, F. D. Synchronicity: The Marriage of Matter and Psyche, Paris, 2014

Russell, M., Piltdown Man: The Secret Life of Charles Dawson, London, 2003

Siebeck, M. *Forschungen zum Alten Testament* (Trans. T. D. Finlay, London 2005

Münnich, M. *The Cult of Bronze Serpents in Ancient Canaan and Israel* (World Union of Jewish Studies, 2005) pp. 39-56
https://www.jstor.org/stable/23531298

Shaver, D. A. *The Books of Enoch (Complete Collection)* 2017

St John of the Cross, *Dark Night of the Soul*, Trans. P. E Allison, New York, 2003

Swedenborg, E. *Heaven and its Wonders and Hell*, Trans. J.C. Ager, West Chester, 2009

Waite, A.E. *The Holy Kabballah: A study of the Secret Tradition in Israel*, London, 1924

Waite, A. E. The Life of Louis Claude se Saint-Martin, The Unknown Philosopher, and the Substance of his Transcendental Doctrine, London, 1901

Waite, A.E. *The Pictorial Key to the Tarot*, London 1910

Index

Aaron, 8, 28, 29, 61, 108, 176
Adam, 45, 61, 69, 72, 98, 104, 105, 110, 116, 120, 121, 139, 140, 141, 142, 144, 145, 154, 168, 169, 173, 194
Adam Kadmon, 104, 105
Ain el-Qudeirat, 7
Alchemy, 105, 155, 198
Amalekites, 36
Ananias, 115
Apep, 29, 68
Apophenia, 49
Asherah, 89
Assyria, 162
Babylon, 162, 165
Boaz, 94
Book of Man, 5, 7
Brazen Serpent, 2, 5, 6, 7, 9, 10, 14, 18, 24, 32, 34, 38, 66, 68, 77, 87, 92, 98, 121, 124, 145, 170, 172, 180, 191, 195
Bretton Woods, 134, 136
Buddhism, 44
Burroughs, 40, 41, 43, 58, 59, 65
Canaan, 24, 65, 199
Carl Jung, 41, 51
Ceremony, 129
Chardin, 192

Church of All Nations, 91
Church of St Peter in Galicantu, 101
Coatlicue, 83
Daniel, 160, 161
Dante, 21, 48, 91
Dawson, 192
Divine Code, 5, 6, 7, 19, 49, 115, 122, 131, 153, 154, 166, 169, 172, 176, 179, 195
Edom, 8, 9, 125, 140, 170
Eilat, 11, 12
Emanuel, 130, 149
Encausse, 68
Enoch, 109, 110, 199
Eutychus, 117, 118, 124
Ezekiel, 11, 12
Field of Reeds, 129
Four Worlds, 46, 159, 179
Franciscans, 11

Gadrel, 109
Gamaliel, 111, 120
Gematria, 27, 165, 166, 169
Genesis, 21, 39, 45, 99, 139, 179
Gerasa, 128
God, 3, 5, 6, 8, 9, 11, 21, 22, 23, 26, 28, 30, 32, 34, 35, 38, 39, 40, 45, 46, 54, 67, 70, 73, 74, 75, 76, 77, 78, 84, 85, 87, 92, 93, 94, 95, 96, 97, 98, 102, 104, 105, 108, 110, 111, 113, 115, 116, 119, 120, 121, 122, 125, 126, 131, 139, 141, 142, 144, 147, 148, 149, 150, 152, 154, 155, 158, 159, 160, 167, 168, 169, 170, 176, 179, 182, 186
Golden Calf, 61, 108
Hebrews, 7, 8, 9, 21, 25, 28, 30, 31, 61, 67, 68, 72, 73, 74, 85, 86, 96, 107, 108, 121, 122, 125, 131, 140, 153, 155, 166, 167, 170, 185, 191
Hermes, 81, 107, 133
Hermes Trismegistus, 107
Hippocratis Coi Medicorum Omnium, 14
Hittites, 24
I-Ching, 60
Jairus', 126, 128, 130
Jeremiah, 61
John of Patmos, 162
Josephus, 61, 110, 113, 197
Judah, 9, 87, 88, 89
Kabballah, 28, 159, 165, 170, 172, 178, 179, 199
Kērykes, 133, 134
kirlian energy, 123
Konstantin, 123
Korotkov, 123, 198
Lamed, 16
Lanza, 186, 187, 198
Lucian, 17
Menorah, 181, 183, 184
Mercy Seat, 34, 35
Meribah, 7
Mesmer, 190
Metallurgy, 26
Minoans, 24
Miriam, 7
Mishnah, 36, 77, 78, 181, 198
Moses, 2, 7, 8, 9, 10, 12, 13, 19, 21, 22, 23, 25, 26, 28, 29, 31, 32, 34, 35, 36, 38, 39, 40, 72, 73, 74, 75, 82, 85, 87, 92, 98, 99, 104, 108, 120, 131, 140, 141, 160, 168, 169, 172, 196, 197

Mount Hor, 8
Mount Horeb, 22, 26, 34, 75, 108, 160
Mount Nebo, 11
Nagas, 109
Nebuchadnezzar, 160
Negev, 8, 11
Nehushtan, 2, 3, 6, 9, 11, 12, 13, 14, 18, 23, 28, 34, 36, 38, 39, 56, 66, 68, 70, 73, 76, 78, 82, 85, 86, 87, 88, 89, 90, 91, 92, 93, 96, 99, 101, 102, 107, 110, 115, 121, 122, 124, 131, 132, 135, 145, 147, 149, 151, 154, 155, 156, 157, 159, 160, 161, 168, 170, 176, 190, 194
Nephilim, 109
Nicodemus, 91, 92, 93, 95, 96, 97, 99, 102, 105, 172
Ningishzida, 82
Noah's Flood, 169
Number, 3, 40, 52, 73, 185, 197
Nun, 37
Omar Garrison, 59
Osiris, 107
Ouroboros, 54, 185
Pasqually, 1, 139, 140, 141, 142, 144, 146, 150, 157, 198
Pool of Bethesda, 168
Pools of Siloam, 168
prima materia, 23, 26, 37, 121, 137, 140, 160, 185, 189
Priya Hemenway, 132
Pulsa Denura, 71, 73
Pythagoras, 53, 54
Pythagoreans, 42, 54, 55, 56, 150, 158, 184
Qadesh, 7
Quetzalcoatl, 55, 82, 84
Rameses, 22
Red Sea, 11, 31, 33, 178
Red Spitting Cobra, 86
Revelation, 42, 62, 162, 163
Roman Empire, 162
Rosicrucians, 54
Sacred Geometry, 54
Sam Parnia, 122
Samaria, 82
Sargon, 22
Sefer HaRazim, 71
Sennacherib, 88
serpent, 2, 6, 9, 10, 14, 17, 18, 19, 23, 26, 28, 29, 31, 32, 35, 36, 38, 39, 42, 54, 68, 70, 73, 74, 82, 83, 85, 86, 87, 88, 90, 92, 99, 105, 107, 108, 110, 131, 132, 135, 150, 151, 157, 160, 161, 162, 168, 181, 190, 196
Serpent, 3, 6, 13, 23, 38, 99, 105, 125,

130, 141, 142, 168, 169, 170
Sigmund Freud, 49
St John of the Cross, 97, 199
St. Paul, 61, 104, 114, 122, 124
Stahl, 189, 190
Sword of Moses, 72
Synchronicity, 49, 52, 198
Tarot, 14, 16, 68, 199
Tau, 10, 11, 12, 14, 17, 124, 172
Teilhard, 192, 193, 194, 195
Thoth, 22, 107
Thutmose, 22
Tiresias, 107, 184
Tlaloc, 84
Tree of Knowledge, 39, 77, 106, 142, 163, 181
Tree of Knowledge of Good and Evil, 39, 77, 106, 142, 163, 181
Tree of Life, 29, 39, 70, 77, 82, 92, 131, 151, 160, 163, 170, 171, 173, 179
Trinosophia, 1, 3, 162, 198
twenty-three enigma, 40, 157
Uzza, 38
vesica piscis, 39, 56, 102, 185
Vesica Piscis, 55, 158
Wadjet, 25, 107
Waite, 15
Waite, A.E, 199
Waters of Strife, 7
Weighing of the Heart, 84, 129
Xiuhcoatl, 23, 74
Zohar, 77, 182

www.ingramcontent.com/pod-product-compliance
Lightning Source LLC
Chambersburg PA
CBHW072007110526
44592CB00012B/1231